SUCCESSFUL PUBLIC SPEAKING

SUCCESSFUL PUBLIC SPEAKING

RAYMOND HULL

arco

New York

808.5

Published by ARCO PUBLISHING COMPANY, INC.
219 Park Avenue South, New York, N.Y. 10003

Copyright © Raymond Hull, 1971

All Rights Reserved

Library of Congress Number 74-127369

ISBN 0-668-02395-3

Printed in the United States of America

Contents

SUCCESSFUL PUBLIC SPEAKING

1. The Nature of Public Speaking

Mend your speech a little, lest you may mar your fortunes.

WILLIAM SHAKESPEARE

Would you like to make more money, to win promotion, to improve your standing in your job, business or profession?

Would you like to develop self-confidence, to the point where you can face an audience—even a hostile audience—of hundreds or thousands and calmly, smilingly, effectively, expound your opinions? Would you enjoy feeling this unshakable self-confidence carry over into your private life, into vocational, family and social situations?

Have you some political, religious, economic or artistic beliefs that you want to propagate? Would you like the power to influence other people, and have them accept and act upon your suggestions?

Are you interested in self-development, in broadening your education, in making your knowledge more accessible, more serviceable, in letting other people know what you know, in becoming recognized as an authority?

Do you wish to obtain office in a club, fraternal organization or trade union? Would you like to stand for election to public office?

Would you like to meet people and go to places that are at present inaccessible to you—to broaden your social horizons?

All these goals can be achieved through the art of public speaking.

Most people are called on to speak from time to time, at weddings, social events and meetings of various kinds. Have you ever been so called, and felt obliged, blushing and stammering, to refuse? Have you ever, against your better judgment, accepted the

1

invitation and made a fool of yourself because you did not know
how to speak? Then you have realized that public speaking is not
as easy as it looks when it is done by a good speaker.

What is the problem? Why is it that any reasonably intelligent
person who wants to make a speech—and who, after all, has been
"speaking" from infancy—cannot deliver a public speech simply
by jumping to his feet.

It is because there are radical differences between public speaking and ordinary conversation. Let us examine those points of
difference: they will guide us in planning and carrying out our
program.

1. Conversation is a flow of ideas from one person to another,
or to a few people. Public speaking is a flow of ideas from one
speaker to a large audience.

2. Conversation consists (or should consist) of a more or less
equal exchange of words between the participants. Public speaking
consists of a one-way flow of words from the speaker to the audience.

3. In conversation the speakers are close to each other. In public speaking the distance from the speaker to the front row of the
audience is usually measured in yards. The rearmost listeners in
a big hall may be so far away that the speaker can scarcely distinguish individual faces.

4. Conversation is usually conducted at low volume. The public
speaker must produce his words loudly, so as to be heard by everyone in the hall.

5. Conversation usually proceeds at a fairly rapid pace. A public speaker, to cope with the receptive abilities of crowds, and with
the acoustics of large buildings, must speak fairly slowly.

6. Much conversation is conducted with a slurred, indistinct
vocal technique. The public speaker must produce his words clearly
and articulately.

7. In conversation, sentence structure and thought arrangement are often disorganized. In public speech, sentences and
thoughts must be systematically arranged.

8. Conversation is often aimless: the speakers are in effect only
making polite noises, to demonstrate their goodwill to one another.
A public speech must have a purpose, and every word, pause, facial
expression and gesture should contribute toward the achievement
of that purpose.

9. Conversation is often weak and indecisive: partly through lack of thought, partly through politeness, the speakers do not say what they mean. A good speech is forceful and decisive; it leaves the listener in no doubt as to the speaker's meaning.

10. The participants in a conversation usually know each other. Much of what they say is meaningful to them, but incomprehensible to strangers. The public speaker often has to address strangers: all that he says must be understood by everyone in the audience.

11. Conversation is usually informal—the speakers sit, stand, move about, eat, drink and smoke as they speak; they look at one another or not, as they please. A public speech is a formal occasion —the speaker stands, while the listeners sit silently in rows, gazing fixedly at him (that is, as long as he holds their attention!)

Let us look at a passage of conversation, and then see how the same information would be conveyed by a public speaker. Imagine the words being delivered at low volume, rapidly and indistinctly.

Conversation

Ya know, Fred, what we were sayin' th' other day 'bout Jack 'n' Betty 'n' all that? Well, listen to this, now. Jack finally made it . . . got the green light. Course, I always thought he would, but it couldn't 've worked out better if I'd planned it m'self.

Notice that, although the other party to this conversation may have understood the news, we do not. Now look at a passage from a public speech. Imagine the words being delivered loudly, slowly and clearly.

Public Speech

Ladies and gentlemen, I have a piece of good news for you, concerning Mr. and Mrs. Jack Jones, two long-time, faithful members of the Ourtown Civic Betterment Society. Jack has received a well-deserved promotion to the head office of the Intergalactic Milk Shake Company, and leaves for New York at the end of the month. I'm sure I speak for us all in offering Jack and Betty our very best wishes for the future. Ourtown's loss is New York's gain.

Notice that everybody—not only the people who know Jack and Betty Jones—can understand this announcement.

To sum up this point, we can say that public speaking is conversation *enlarged, clarified* and *directed*.

You can learn the art of enlarging, clarifying and directing your conversation so as to turn it into public speech. Unless there exists some gross defect of intelligence or of the vocal organs, anyone can become a competent speaker. Most people can become good speakers.

I emphasize the idea of *becoming* a good speaker. It is an art that must be learned. There is no such thing as a born public speaker. If you examine the careers of so-called born speakers, you will find that they were exposed in youth to a great deal of oratory, either from the pulpit or the platform, and that they learned to speak well by imitation.

So you can learn to speak in public. There is nothing difficult or mysterious about the art. It requires study and practice, but you will find that the results are worth the effort.

How to Use this Book

If you simply read this book, it will help you to appreciate the technique of the speakers you hear. It will heighten your enjoyment of their speeches, but it will not make you into a speaker. Twenty readings of the book would not enable you to spring to your feet and make a good speech. *You must practice.*

Public speaking is one of the performing arts, like acting and singing: it involves auditory, visual and emotional relationships between the speaker and the audience. Solitary practice is beneficial for some aspects of your development as a speaker (breathing, voice, phrasing, etc.), but it is not enough. You must obtain frequent practice *in front of an audience*.

The best way to get this practice is by enrollment in a public speaking class. There you will have the helpful criticism and correction, and the good example, of the instructor. There you will have a sympathetic audience of fellow-students. You will be able to use this book as a useful supplement to the lectures and practice sessions, and as a refresher and guide to further development once the course is over.

If you cannot find such a class, then organize a group of people who are interested in learning to speak in public, and use this book as your teacher. It contains useful hints on conducting training sessions.

If you cannot organize such a group, seize every opportunity of speaking before an audience. If need be, join several organizations where you will have this opportunity. Note your difficulties and go back repeatedly to this book for hints on overcoming them.

If you are teaching a course on public speaking, this book will serve as a useful text.

Summary

The ability to speak publicly can
1. Increase your income.
2. Give you self-confidence.
3. Propagate your views.
4. Broaden your education.
5. Enrich your social life.
Public speaking differs radically from conversation.
It is conversation enlarged, clarified and directed.
Public speaking is a performing art.
To learn it, practice *before an audience*.

2. Preliminary Technique

Practice is the best of all instructors.
PUBLILIUS SYRUS

You cannot learn to speak without actually speaking, so every member of the class or group should speak to an audience at every session. This chapter offers technical information that will help you to begin practical work at once. Some points mentioned in this chapter will be dealt with more fully later in the book, but there is enough detail here to lead you into making an interesting and instructive short speech.

This is as good a time as any to point out that the suggestions offered in this book are not cast-iron rules. Public speaking is an art—an intensely personal art—and as such it has few inviolable rules. You will no doubt hear good speakers who omit some things that I recommend, and who do some things that I disparage. The test of a speaking technique is its effect upon the audience. If a speaker produces the desired effect upon his audience, then *for him,* and *for that audience,* the technique is sound.

But the methods described in this book are well-tested: they are easy and quick; they cannot lead the beginner astray; and they will work with most speakers and most audiences. So I suggest that you give these methods a fair trial. If, after gaining considerable experience, you wish to modify them, you can always do so.

6

Methods of Delivery

There are four methods of delivering a prepared speech. The worst is mentioned first, the best last.

Reading

Make up your mind from the first that you are not going to slip into the faint-hearted, ineffective and time-wasting habit of reading a script instead of making a speech.

The habit is faint-hearted because it usually implies that the reader lacks confidence in his knowledge of the subject and his ability to discuss it. He is afraid to frame his thoughts into words on the spot and present them to the audience.

The habit is ineffective because, unless the speaker has an uncommon degree of writing ability, his script will sound like something out of a book, and not like a speech. Moreover, unless he is an unusually good reader, he will bore the audience. The listeners soon tire of seeing the top of the reader's head and hearing the drone of his voice.

The habit is time wasting because there should be no need for you to write out every word of your speech. A speaker's business is to train himself so that he can clearly and fluently transform *ideas* into *words*.

There are four conditions in which reading is acceptable.

1. If you are an unusually important person—say a high government official—making a statement so vital that not one syllable of it may be varied—say a major policy statement or a declaration of war—then it may be advisable to read from a script. (Many people who are not very important, issuing statements of no great significance, flatter themselves that they fall within this category, and so read when they would do better to speak.)

2. If you are speaking on radio, and precise timing is required, a script may be necessary.

3. If you want to include in a speech a quotation from some printed work, it will be desirable to read the quotation, so that you get it right.

4. Reading is useful in class for certain exercises, to develop self-confidence and to train the voice.

But let it stand as a general rule that speeches should be spoken and not read.

Recitation

This is the most time-wasting method of all. The reciter not only must write his speech, but also he must toil for days or weeks to memorize it. The method has other disadvantages.

Reciting is not *speaking*. Unless the reciter is a good actor, it will be obvious to the audience that he is not thinking as he speaks, but is only parroting something he has learned.

As in the case of the reader, the reciter's script—unless he is a first-class speech-writer—sounds bookish, even though it is recited and not read.

The reciter is harassed, all through the preparation period, and through the recitation itself, by the fear of forgetting or transposing part of the script. This fear produces muscular tension which is apparent to the audience, and which often impairs the quality of the reciter's voice.

Reciting, in my view, has only one point in its favor: the reciter can look at the audience all the time, so his performance is less boring for them than a reading. But this by no means offsets the serious disadvantages of the method: reciting should never be used as a substitute for speaking.

Memorized Headings

The speaker does not write a complete script, but plans his speech in outline and then memorizes the headings. The labor involved is obviously much less than with reciting or reading.

Moreover, this speaker is actually *speaking*, transforming ideas into words, there on the platform, in front of the audience. This gives the speech a spontaneity and persuasive quality which can scarcely be obtained by reciting or reading.

The speaker has only a few things to remember. For example, suppose you were using this technique to speak on "Methods of Delivering a Speech." You would write and memorize something like this:

Four Methods

1. *Reading*
   The worst
   Faint-hearted
   Ineffective: bookish, boring
   Time wasting
   Four acceptable conditions:
   1) Important
   2) Radio, timing
   3) Long quotes
   4) Exercises
2. *Recitation*
   Most time wasting
   Not *speaking*
   Bookish
   Fear, tension
   Less boring than reading
3. *Memorized Headings*
   Saves time, labor
   Real speaking—spontaneous
   Little to memorize
   Risk forgetting—tension
   Better than reading, reciting
4. *Notes*
   Eliminate fears
   No disadvantages
   Cannot forget or transpose
   Audience doesn't mind
   Increase confidence of speaker
   Increase confidence of audience
   Easiest, best way

This is not much to memorize—about seventy words—and it would easily form the basis of a ten-minute speech of twelve hundred words.

Yet headings such as these are not the easiest material to remember; there is a risk of forgetting or transposing some of the items. The speaker knows this, and is bound to suffer some degree of fear and tension.

If this method is carried off successfully, it gives better results than either reading or reciting. Still I do not recommend it.

Notes

The beginning speaker suffers much from fear: fear of not making himself heard, fear of the gaze of the audience, fear of making grammatical mistakes, and so on. Why on earth should he burden himself further with the fear of forgetting what he wants to say?

By speaking from notes, he eliminates that fear. Speaking from notes has all the advantages and none of the risks of using memorized headings. Indeed, the method—correctly used—has no disadvantages at all. The speaker is sure that he cannot forget or transpose any part of his speech, and so gives his whole attention to framing and delivering it as well as he knows how.

An audience does not mind seeing the speaker use notes. They have not come to see him give a memory demonstration, but to hear him make a speech.

Adequate notes increase the speaker's self-confidence and give the audience greater confidence in the speaker.

I unhesitatingly advise you to make and use notes. It is the easiest way and the best way to speed your development as a speaker.

Handling the Notes

1. Don't try to hide your notes. I have seen a speaker carrying notes on a card about two inches square, held in the palm of his left hand. From time to time he would raise the hand and surreptitiously look into it for his next idea. I have heard of speakers writing notes or mnemonic symbols on their fingernails. You need play no such tricks on your audience. Use cards or sheets of paper; write or type your notes big enough to be read easily, and consult them unashamedly.

2. If there is a lectern of convenient height on the platform, put your notes on it and leave them alone, except for turning the pages.

3. If there is just a table on the platform, lay the notes on it

only if the writing is big enough for you to read without bowing your head.

4. If you cannot read your notes as they lie on the table, hold them in one hand. Let the hand that holds the notes hang naturally at your side for most of the time. When you want to refer to the notes, raise them high enough so that you can read them without bending your neck.

5. A right-handed speaker will find it most convenient to hold the notes in his left hand, and keep the right free for gesturing. If you are left-handed, hold the notes in your right hand.

6. An alternative method of handling the notes is to hold them most of the time with both hands, in front of the body, at waist level. When raising the notes to read, use one hand only, and let the other fall naturally to your side. This method is a graceful one for a woman.

7. The easiest format is to have all your notes on one card or one piece of paper. For lengthy speeches you may need more space. If you have a number of cards or sheets, don't begin with them all in your hand and then lay each one down on the table as you are done with it. This procedure gives some members of the audience an irresistible desire to keep counting the sheets you still have in your hand! They concentrate on this counting and so pay less attention to what you are saying. Therefore, as each sheet or card is done with, put it beneath the others and keep the whole bundle in your hand.

8. Don't peer at your notes while you are speaking. Read the first note on your sheet. Speak until you have fully expressed the idea which that note represents. *Pause,* look at the second note, and speak about that idea. Pause again, look at the third note, and so on. Don't be afraid to pause! You have just imparted an idea to the audience; and they will be quite content to think about it for a second or two while you glance at your notes.

The Speaking Voice

We shall fully discuss voice development in Chapter 10, but here are some hints that will start you in the right direction.

1. Speak loudly—*much louder* than you do in ordinary conversation.

Holding a practice session in a school classroom, I advise students, "Don't be satisfied with speaking loudly enough to fill this room. Imagine you are in an auditorium, facing three hundred people. Then imagine that in the back row of that auditorium there is a deaf lady. Speak loudly enough to make her hear."

I shall often refer to that deaf lady in the back row. The more you think of her and direct your efforts toward making her hear and understand and enjoy what you are saying, the better speaker you will become.

The one rule that no speaker can dare violate is, *Make yourself heard.*

It is better to speak too loudly than too softly. Make yourself heard, and you have a firm foundation on which to build your speaking technique. Fail to make yourself heard, and keen intelligence, penetrating thought and elegant phraseology all go for nothing. So *speak as loudly as you can without shouting.*

2. Speak clearly. The mumblings and slurrings of everyday conversation would seriously impede your communication with the audience, especially with that deaf lady in the back row. Make every word crisp and precise. Give every vowel and consonant its full value. Pay particular attention to the *ends* of your words. Speak with an *exaggerated* correctness and clarity.

This style of speech, admittedly, would sound pompous and affected in ordinary conversation, but it is necessary, and it sounds effective, on the platform.

Try hard, practice, and learn to articulate clearly. *It is impossible to speak too clearly.*

3. Speak slowly. A crowd of people cannot absorb ideas as fast as can an individual. You cannot afford to rush ahead and leave some of your audience behind, uncomprehending. The speed of the fleet is that of the slowest ship. The speed of the speaker must be such that the deaf lady in the back row can follow him with comfort.

Most people find that they have to speak much below their ordinary conversational pace. The maximum for platform work is 150 words a minute. Even better is 120 words a minute. Some first-class speakers, accustomed to working with big audiences, deliver 100 words a minute, or less.

So *force yourself to slow down.* Deliver the words more slowly than you would in conversation. Make the pauses for phrase endings, sentence endings and breaths longer than you do in conversation.

It is better to speak too slowly than too quickly.

4. Watch your audience. You will see by their head movements and facial expressions if they are finding it difficult to hear and follow you. If you see heads cocked sideways in a strained "listening" posture, speak more loudly and more clearly. If you see puzzled frowns, or looks of blank incomprehension, speak more slowly.

Basic Speech Structure

The typical speech consists of three parts, the *opening,* the *body (middle,* or *discussion,* as this part is sometimes called) and the *conclusion.* The opening introduces the subject, the body expounds it, and the conclusion reviews it.

Another way of expressing this three-fold structure is:

1. Tell them what you're going to tell them.
2. Tell them.
3. Tell them what you've told them.

In the opening, you capture the attention of the audience and direct it toward the subject. You arouse their interest by showing briefly how the subject concerns them. The opening is usually short —about one-tenth of the speech.

In the body you enumerate your main points, impart the bulk of your information, marshal your evidence, or make your main appeal to the audience. The body usually occupies about four-fifths of your total time.

In the conclusion you briefly recapitulate your main points and present one strong, final thought that you wish to leave with the audience. It is best to keep the conclusion brief—not more than a tenth of the speech. A dragged-out, "never-ending" finish, where the speaker seems not to conclude, but simply rambles on until he runs out of ideas, will kill the effect of an otherwise strong speech.

So, when you have presented that strong, final idea, *stop at once.*

Do not end with the phrase, "I thank you." It is anticlimactic; it weakens the effect of your strong concluding sentence. It is unnecessary. If you have done your job properly, it is the audience who should thank you!

(There is one situation in which "I thank you" is sometimes held to be acceptable: at a meeting where you were not supposed to be speaking, but have asked, and been granted, permission to say a few words. Even then, it would be better to express your thanks at the beginning, rather than at the end of your speech. ''Mr. Chairman, thank you for giving me permission to address the meeting . . . . etc.'')

Later we shall see how to build speeches of many kinds on this basic plan. There is no better way of arranging a speech; it is the only way you need to know.

Just Before You Speak

If you are sitting on the platform, awaiting your turn to speak, keep your eyes on the chairman or on whoever is speaking at the moment, or else on the floor. Don't gaze around the audience yet. You may distract some of their attention from the person who is speaking. This is discourteous.

If you have been sitting in front with the audience waiting for your turn to speak, as soon as the chairman calls you forward, approach the platform *with your eyes turned toward the ground*. Don't look up at the chairman and don't gaze around at the audience, or you run the risk of tripping over a mat or falling up the steps of the platform. An accident like this will ruin your speech before you begin it.

Carry your notes in your hand. Thus you make sure that you have not left them at your seat, and you do not have to fumble for them in your pocket or handbag after you get on the platform.

The Salutation

When the chairman (or the person who has introduced you) calls on you to speak, stand and wait silently until he is seated again. *Never rush to deliver your first words.*

If you are going to use the lectern, move slowly toward it and place your notes on it in silence. If you are already in the position from which you intend to speak, simply stand and place your notes on the table, or hold them in your hand.

At this stage, the people do not want to hear your voice; they want a chance to look at you for a few moments and size you up.

When the chairman or introducer has sat down, and all other movement on the platform and in the audience has ceased, look at the chairman. Give a slight smile (unless the occasion is an unusually solemn one) and say, "Mr. Chairman."

A slight bow or gesture toward the chairman is permissible at this time, if you feel comfortable doing it. It is not essential.

If, as sometimes happens, the chairman is right behind you, do not turn all the way around so that the audience sees the back of your head. Simply turn your head about half-way around and say the two words in that position.

If a woman is in the chair, say, "Madam Chairman." As illogical as it sounds, this is the accepted expression. Or, if the presiding official has some other title, use it: "Mr. President," "Mr. Speaker," "Mr. Moderator," and so on.

Then pause and turn to the audience. Gaze first to the left, sweep your gaze to the right, then back to the center, and say *slowly,* "Ladies . . . (pause one second) . . . and Gentlemen."

A slight smile is appropriate at this point, too, except on very solemn occasions.

If the audience is all ladies or all gentlemen, you will of course say "Ladies" or "Gentlemen" as the case may be. If there is one lady or one gentleman in an audience of the opposite sex, do not create embarrassment by saying, "Madam and Gentlemen" or "Ladies and Sir." Use the regular expression "Ladies and Gentlemen."

If the occasion is informal, or if you have particularly warm feelings toward the audience, you can say, "Mr. Chairman, friends . . ." or "Mr. Chairman, my friends . . ."

"Mr. Chairman, fellow-citizens," is a useful salutation for a political meeting.

Some organizations have special forms of address that are used at their meetings. You will, of course, use such a special form when it is appropriate.

"Mr. Chairman, Ladies and Gentlemen" is usually enough of a salutation. Don't run through a long list of names or titles such as, "Mr. Chairman, fellow-speakers, Senator, Mr. Mayor, distinguished guests, committee members, Ladies and Gentlemen."

(But if several preceding speakers have used some such formula you might as well follow suit, lest you seem to be correcting them by doing something different.)

After the salutation, pause two seconds, then go into the opening of your speech.

Deliver the salutation *loudly,* and *clearly. Never rush it.* If you mutter or hurry the salutation, you give the audience the idea that you are nervous. If you do it loudly and clearly, you will make them feel that you are confident.

Properly done, the salutation rivets the attention of the audience on you.

You can force yourself to speak the salutation slowly by counting silently between the words. "Mr. Chairman (one . . . two . . . three . . .) Ladies (. . . one . . .) and Gentlemen (. . . one . . . two . . .) and into the opening.

If you are chairman, or if you are the first speaker on a program without a chairman, you can quiet and settle the audience simply by saying, "Ladies and Gentlemen" loudly and slowly.

Summary

Regularly practice speaking to an audience.

Don't read your speeches.

Don't memorize and recite your speeches.

Don't waste time memorizing speech headings.

Speak from notes: the sure-fire method.

Handle your notes confidently: don't try to hide them.

Three essential vocal qualities are:

    1. Ample power

    2. Perfect clarity

    3. Unhurried pace

The basic speech structure includes the opening, body, and conclusion.

Don't end a speech with "I thank you."

Stand silent, briefly, before delivering the Salutation.

Speak the Salutation loudly, clearly, and slowly.

Exercises

1. If the members of the group do not already know each other, here is a good topic for the first speech. Let each student introduce

himself, tell something about himself, and briefly explain why he wants to learn public speaking.

It is worth emphasizing that the speech should be personal. Don't talk in general terms about the benefits of public speaking, but give your speech an individual quality.

Although you will not make a long, elaborate speech on the first attempt, your speech should have the following correct form:

Opening—State your name and any other information you care to give.

Body—Give your reasons for wanting to learn public speaking.

Conclusion—Give a summary, and a strong, constructive idea.

Here are two short speeches that illustrate what can be done with this exercise.

Mr. Chairman, Ladies and Gentlemen, my name is Laurence Neuman.

I was born in Philadelphia and grew up there. When I left school I went into the hardware business, first as a sales clerk, selling nuts and bolts, kitchen knives, paint and so on.

When I got more experience, I worked in bigger stores, as department manager, in hardware, and in major appliances.

Three years ago, I moved to this area and set up my own hardware store. Some of you may know it, on the Hillcrest Shopping Plaza.

The store's doing fairly well, but I think it could do even better if I was a better speaker—if I could talk to the customers better and explain to them about the various things they might want to buy.

Another thing: I've recently joined the Kinsmen's Club, and I'd like to be able to get up at the meetings and deliver a speech as well as some of the other members can.

So that's why I want to learn public speaking. I've enjoyed this first session so far, and I'm looking forward to getting ahead fast.

Delivered at a moderate pace, this speech will last for two minutes. That is enough for a first effort.

Here is the other sample speech. Again, note the three-fold form: Opening, Body and Conclusion.

Mr. Chairman, Ladies and Gentlemen, my name is Bernice Harrison.

I was born and raised in this city, and went to school right here in this building. I worked several years as a stenographer, then married my boss.

I'm now fully occupied keeping house for my husband and three children—two girls and one boy.

All the children are in school, so naturally I'm involved with the PTA. Well, I used to just sit through those PTA meetings, too shy to open my mouth.

Once, when they were all getting excited about the new school lunchroom, I did jump up and try to say something, but I was so nervous that I don't know what I said. Whatever it was, I must have put it badly, because I certainly didn't seem to get my point over to the other members.

Anyway, I began to feel I'd like to be able to speak properly. My husband is all in favor of it. He's a good speaker himself. So he's keeping house tonight while I'm having a good time here.

That's just about what I want from the public speaking course. I hope I'll have the perseverance to follow through with it.

This, too, would be about a two-minute speech.

2. Another good exercise for the first session is to have each student read a short item from a newspaper and comment briefly on it.

The reading is a useful exercise in the early stages.

(1) It gives the student something to do with his hands.

(2) It gets him used to the sound of his own voice speaking loudly.

(3) For part of the time, it keeps his eyes off the audience, and so mitigates his stage fright.

In this exercise, too, the speech should have the correct three-part form.

Opening—Briefly indicate what you are going to read.

Body—Read the clipping and, if possible, offer some further facts concerning the subject, from your own knowledge.

Conclusion—Sum up, and make some pointed comment on the subject. What does it mean? What will it lead to? What should be done about it?

Here is a typical example.

Mr. Chairman, Ladies and Gentlemen, I have here a clipping from the *Galaxia County Courier* of today's date.

MILKY RIVER BRIDGE COLLAPSES

At 3 a.m. Monday morning, the Milky River Bridge collapsed and fell into the thirty-foot deep water.

Fortunately, no traffic was on the bridge, although an automobile driven by John Herman of 3218 Sunshine Valley Road narrowly missed plunging into the gap.

"I was coming home from work," said Herman, "and heard this terrific rumble, and saw the span just disappear from out the beam of my headlights."

"Luckily my brakes were in good order, and I managed to stop in time."

Charles Wingate, County Engineer, said, "We can't guess at the cause of the collapse till we make a thorough examination of the wreckage."

"I've driven over that bridge often, and walked over it, too. 'Specially when walking, you could feel it shake to the traffic. I always assumed it was just normal vibration, but apparently it wasn't.

"We should be thankful that the bridge didn't go down at a rush-hour and drown scores of people.

"All bridges are supposed to be tested from time to time by expert engineers. I suppose this one was, too, but the tests couldn't have shown the weakness.

"It seems to me, this accident shows that you can't afford to put too much faith in the so-called experts."

3. This is an exercise in fluency to be done at home. Sometime toward the end of each day, make a speech telling what you have done that day. Begin with the regular salutation, and force yourself to talk for at least three minutes *without stopping*. It is important that you keep talking. If you are momentarily at a loss for new ideas, force yourself to repeat in different words what you said in the previous sentence, and keep on rephrasing the same idea until the next idea occurs to you.

This exercise is best performed in solitude, in a full-speaking voice. You can do it as you drive home from work. If you cannot get enough privacy to speak aloud, do the exercise in a whisper. (Lock yourself in the bathroom for three minutes if need be.)

3. Preparing the Speech

It is a bad plan that admits of no modification.
PUBLILIUS SYRUS

In emergencies, you may have to speak with little or no preparation but, whenever you can, plan your speeches well in advance. Unplanned speeches tend to ramble; often they make no definite impression on the audience, and so fail to carry out the speaker's purpose. Let us see how best to prepare a speech.

Define Your Theme

If a speaker has failed to define his theme, after the speech people will say, "I couldn't make out what he was driving at."

To ensure that the audience knows what you are driving at, be clear about it yourself. Define your theme. Write it out, in one brief sentence. Imagine that you could not get to the hall to deliver your speech, and had to distill the whole substance of it into a short telegram.

The theme is sometimes called the *aim* or *purpose* of the speech. It is a concise statement of what you hope to achieve by the speech.

The theme may or may not be implicit in the subject of the speech. Suppose, for example, your subject is "Abolish Capital Punishment," "Clean Up Our City Streets," or "Drive Safely and Stay Alive." Then in each instance theme and subject are identical.

But suppose your subject is "Adult Education"; then the theme is not apparent. You could choose any one of many themes, all relevant to that subject. For example, "Adult education programs benefit the whole community," "Adult education wastes the taxpayers' money," "The humorous side of night school," or "How adult education raised me from failure to success." If I were assigned that subject, I might take as a theme, "My experiences as a night-school teacher."

Or suppose the subject is "Liquor Legislation." Your theme might be "Liquor sale and consumption should be more closely controlled," "Government should not meddle with the citizens' drinking habits," "Liquor taxes are too high," "Drunk driving should be more severely penalized," "The legal age for liquor purchase should be raised," "What this country needs is Prohibition," or "Liquor taxes should be used to support alcoholism research and treatment."

There are four types of theme.

Type 1. To Impart Information

The life of the old-time cowboy was nothing like cowboy movies.
How I tamed a wild timber-wolf.
The search for Captain Kidd's treasure.
The life and work of Leonardo da Vinci.
The discovery of the Dead Sea Scrolls.

There is little room for doubt or dispute on such themes. You simply impart the information in an interesting way. The audience accepts it and, you hope, remembers some of it.

Type 2. To Inspire Belief

I want you to believe that flying saucers are from outer space.
I want you to believe that inheritance taxes are unfair.
I want you to believe that proportional representation is a fair, practical system.
I want you to believe in Christian Science (or Buddhism, or Socialism, or Monarchy, etc.)
I want you to believe in my interpretation of the signficance of the Dead Sea Scrolls.

With regard to themes of this type, there may be room for difference of opinion. So you will present arguments and evidence, making a systematic effort to convert the audience to a belief in your theme.

Type 3. To Arouse Emotion

You should feel pity for the starving children of India.
You should feel shame at the dirty condition of our city.
You should feel glad that you live in a democracy.
You should feel dismay at the rising tide of crime.
You should feel enthusiasm for our political party (or school, or football club, etc.)
You should feel mirth at the battle of the sexes in marriage.
You should feel pleasure at the marriage of Tom and Betty.

This type of theme demands more from the audience than mere belief. A belief need not involve any emotion. For example, most educated people believe that the earth is round, and accept the idea dispassionately (although people used to get highly emotional about it!) People tend to feel emotional mostly about matters that closely affect them.

Type 4. To Obtain Action

Vote for me, for Mayor of this city.
Quit smoking to avoid lung cancer.
Prepare a speech for the next session of the public speaking class.
Give a donation to the Civic Beautification Fund.
Pledge support for one hungry Asian child.
Reduce your weight to lengthen your life.

This type of theme takes the audience a stage beyond arousing emotion, to *doing something* about the emotion.

To sum up, then: If your subject has not already done it for you, *define your theme*. If at first you cannot do so, keep thinking and keep jotting down notes until you can. Define the theme accurately and concisely, and *write it down*.

Know Your Audience

You cannot make an effective speech unless you know something—the more, the better—about the audience. You cannot take the same speech and deliver it *effectively* to several different audiences.

I emphasize "effectively." Effective delivery is not simply a matter of speaking loudly, clearly and slowly—although making yourself heard and understood is the necessary first stage. Your speech is effective only *if it produces the desired effect on your audience.*

With Type 1 themes, the desired effect is that the audience shall understand and retain the information you offer.

With Type 2 themes, the desired effect is that the audience shall be converted to your belief; or, if they already hold that belief, that their existing belief shall be reinforced.

With Type 3 themes, the desired effect is the arousal of emotion in the audience.

With Type 4 themes, the desired effect is that the audience shall be led to take the recommended action.

The final effect is all that matters—everything must be contrived to produce that effect.

Let us express the process graphically.

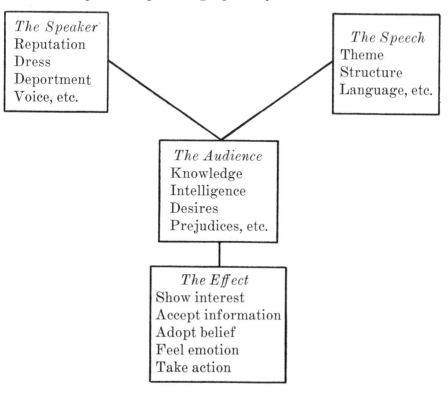

The speech and the speaker both produce various effects on the audience. The speech alone would produce some effect if printed in a newspaper, and read silently by individuals sitting at home. But, if the speaker is doing his job properly, the effect will be made more powerful, more certain, and more long-lasting by his presence before the audience and by his personal style of delivery.

To do his job properly the speaker must adapt his speech and his method of delivering it, to the audience.

For example, suppose you had to speak about "Electric Automobiles"; you would not make the same speech to an audience of auto mechanics as you would to an audience of auto owners and drivers.

Why? Because the two groups have different knowledge, interests, beliefs and prejudices on the subject.

The mechanics naturally believe it is right and necessary that automobiles should break down—the oftener the better.

They will be interested in such questions as these:

How will the coming of electric automobiles affect my job?

What new skills, tools and equipment shall I have to acquire?

How much of my present investment in skill, tools and equipment must be scrapped?

Will electric automobiles require as much repair work as gasoline-powered ones do?

The ordinary automobile owner-driver naturally believes it is wrong and unnecessary that his automobile should break down. He desires a maintenance-free vehicle.

He is interested in such questions as these:

What will be the initial cost of the electric auto?

How long will it last?

How much will it cost per mile to run?

How far will it go, at what speed, without charging or refueling?

How safe is it?

Will it require different driving techniques?

In each instance your theme might be the same—you should feel enthusiasm for the development and marketing of the electric automobile. Nevertheless, the two speeches would have to be radically different, because the two audiences are different.

So, to prepare a speech without a preliminary study of the audience is to risk failure and disappointment. Many speakers make this audience-analysis unconsciously. They just use material and techniques that they feel will be "suitable." You can get better results by a deliberate analysis of the audience, asking yourself such questions as these:

How many people will probably be there?

What proportions of men, women and children?

What will be their average age?

What will be the extremes of age?

What is their average income?

What are the extremes of income?

Have they any strong common bond? (e.g., all members of a church, club, political party, etc.)

What is their average level of intelligence and education?

What are the extremes of intelligence and education?

What can I safely assume that they know of the subject?

What are their prejudices concerning the subject?

Are they already interested in the subject?

If so, how keenly?

Have they any other relevant prejudices and beliefs?

Have they any special sensitivities which I had better not irritate? (e.g., political, religious, racial, regional, vocational, etc.)

Having analyzed your audience, you may see the need to revise your theme. It is futile to choose a theme and prepare a speech that cannot possibly produce any effect upon the audience.

Suppose you are a staunch teetotaler planning to address an audience consisting of representatives of the liquor industry. It would be futile to deliver a speech with the Type 4 theme, "Swear off alcoholic beverages and join my Total Abstainers' Association." Even if you had the eloquence of an angel, you would fail.

But if you choose a more appropriate theme, "Persuade your firms to make modest contributions toward research into alcoholism," then a well-planned and well-delivered speech might produce the desired effect.

A rule that will help in relating theme to audience is:

Not everything that I would like to say

But *what I can effectively convey.*

Suit the Speech to the Audience

You cannot say everything about a subject—even the smallest subject—in one speech. Beginners often try to do this; the result is a string of generalities that are neither interesting nor informative.

For example:

"The continent of Africa is vast, dark and mysterious to outside observers."

"Every serious-minded citizen must feel alarm as he views the rising tide of crime."

"There is a grave and growing lack of communication between the generations."

Skim over a subject with such vague statements, and you end up having said nothing significant about it.

You might as well try to make a friend familiar with a foreign country by flying him over it at six hundred miles an hour. You would show him more of that country by taking him for a meal in one of its restaurants, and then walking him down a street, with eyes and ears wide open, and camera clicking.

So don't try to skim over the whole of a subject in one speech. My uncle Harry, a clergyman, expressed the idea well: "Don't try to preach the whole gospel in one sermon."

For the best effect, *thoroughly cover a few points*. How do you decide which points to deal with? Ask yourself, "Which aspects of the subject will be most interesting and most helpful *now* to my audience?"

Here is an example. I was recently asked to visit a high school and talk about public speaking to some Grade 10 students. I had one hour, and wanted to spend at least twenty minutes on questions and discussion. It would have been futile to try to cover the entire subject of "Public Speaking" in forty minutes. Questioning the teacher, I found that the class had had no practice in public speaking, and that most of them were nervous at the idea of it. So I chose a Type 4 theme: "Develop self-confidence for speaking in fifteen easy steps."

With students who had, through experience, conquered their initial nervousness, I would have had to choose a different theme.

So don't talk about the whole vast, dark, mysterious continent of Africa—discuss a few points that are relevant to your audience. One example is: "Do you know which of the common products on the shelves of your grocery store come from Africa?"

Don't talk about "the rising tide of crime." One suitable point would be: "In our city, during the past twelve months, car thefts have increased by seven percent, burglaries by eleven percent, and robberies with violence by sixteen percent.''

Don't bemoan ''the growing lack of communication between the generations,'' but say as one of your points, ''You who are mothers and fathers, do you know, *really know*, where your teenage daughter is, who she is with, and what she is doing, at this moment?''

Five points chosen because of their strong appeal to the audience, and thoroughly covered, will make a better speech than a hundred and five generalities.

In the following chapters we shall see in more detail how to apply this principle in the various parts of the speech.

Make the Speech Personal

A good speech is characteristic of the speaker. It is not impersonal like an encyclopedia article; it makes liberal use of the speaker's own experiences and opinions.

To be sure, personal material alone will be inadequate for most speeches—you will usually want to incorporate facts from outside sources. (Chapter 22 discusses research methods.) Yet the speech will seem somewhat dull and colorless unless it reveals something of you, the speaker.

A beginner sometimes feels that it is immodest to thrust his experience and personality on listeners. Not at all! They are listening to you because they want to hear what *you* know and what *you* think. So tell them. They will like you and your speech better for it.

In preparing a speech, then, jot down answers to such questions as these:

What do I know about the subject?

How did I learn it? Who told me? Where? When?

What do I think about the subject?

What experiences have I had, relative to the subject?

Have any of my relations, friends or neighbors had experiences relative to the subject?

These and similar questions will provide you with *material that no other speaker can duplicate*. This personal information will enliven your speech and make it sound more interesting and more authoritative.

Let us return to the subjects we mentioned earlier and see how personal touches might be used.

On Africa: "My earliest ideas about Africa came from looking at and handling a knobkerrie that my uncle Albert kept hanging on the wall of his living room."

On crime: "Last Tuesday evening someone broke into my next door neighbor's home, stole all the cash and jewelry, smashed a hundred and fifty phonograph records, and poured a gallon of green porch paint all over the brown living room carpet."

On communication between the generations: "Yesterday a sixteen-year-old boy said to me, 'I have never, never in my life had one serious, friendly conversation with my father.'"

A member of my night school class, speaking on racial discrimination, said, "I was brought up in the Northwest Territories, in a community where whites were in a minority; and by the time I was nine or ten, I often found myself wishing I was an Indian!"

Selecting Material

In Chapter 2 we discussed the basic speech structure—opening, body and conclusion. We now see the kind of material that should be used to fill out that structure.

1. All material should be relevant to the theme.
2. All material should tend to produce the desired effect.
3. All material should interest the audience.
4. Some of the material should be characteristic of the speaker.
5. The material should just fill the allotted time.

Number 5 is important! The gravest fault a speaker can have is to be inaudible. The next is to speak *too long*. To go on for too long will undo everything you may have accomplished earlier in the speech. Indeed, it may arouse active hostility toward you and the cause you advocate.

It is better to be too brief than too long.

Making Notes

Some speakers make their notes on cards. 4 inches by 6 and 5 inches by 8 are convenient sizes. Others prefer to use paper. 8½ inches by 11 is the largest size you can conveniently handle on the platform. Avoid flimsy, floppy sheets of paper. You cannot control them; they stick together so that you turn over two sheets instead of one; they get crumpled, torn and illegible by the time you reach the platform; and they make a distracting rustle every time you move them. A fairly heavy typing or note paper will be easy to handle.

Whether you write or type your notes, don't crowd the material too closely together, or you will find it hard to read.

Don't put too many details into your notes.

Some speakers write out opening and closing sentences verbatim. But apart from these, the only complete sentences on the sheet should be quotations that are to be read to the audience. Usually you will find that a few words suffice to remind you of each idea you want to express.

For example, suppose I were making notes with a view to using this section of the chapter as part of a speech. The following would be sufficient:

Notes

1. Cards 4 x 6 or 5 x 8
   Paper 8½ x 11
   Not flimsy: uncontrollable
            stick together
            crumpled, torn, illegible
            rustle
   Stiff
2. Space out. Easy to read.
3. Brevity. Open, close, verbatim?
           Quotes
           Reminder of ideas
           Eyes on aud.
4. Number; drop, rearrange.

If you have studied and thought about your subject, such brief notes will be adequate. The notes are not intended to be a copy of the words the audience will hear. They are *reminders of the ideas* that you will be transforming into words as you speak.

Copious, overdetailed notes tempt you to keep your eyes on the paper instead of on the audience.

Number the sheets or cards so that, if you drop them, you can quickly set them in order again.

Rehearsal

There is some difference of opinion about the value of rehearsing a speech. Many speakers do not rehearse at all: that is, they never speak the speech aloud until they deliver it. Others do more or less rehearsal, either alone in front of a mirror, or with a friend for audience and critic.

Advocates of rehearsal urge these points:

1. Rehearsal is a good way for the speaker to get familiar with his material.

2. Rehearsal develops self-confidence.

3. Rehearsal leads to more fluent delivery. By trial and error the speaker smooths out the rough spots in his speech and so gets it in first-class condition for eventual delivery.

4. The friendly listener-critic can often make helpful suggestions.

5. Rehearsal is a means of timing the speech.

On the other hand we have these objections to rehearsal:

1. Proper rehearsal is so time consuming that few people can do it. Little is to be gained by muttering through the speech at two hundred words a minute. Rehearsal, to do any good, must be done at the same speed, and with the same power, that will be used before the audience.

2. Proper rehearsal is tiring.

3. Excessive rehearsal may lead to memorizing the speech. We have already discussed some disadvantages of this procedure.

4. It is hard to find a listener who is friendly enough to sit through rehearsals, and who is at the same time detached enough to criticize frankly and usefully.

5. Even the most conscientious rehearsal is lacking in one important element—the presence of the audience. The mirrored image or the solitary listener is by no means equivalent to the audience that the speaker must face when he delivers the speech.

Some speakers rehearse with a tape recorder. This lets the speaker play back his speech and be his own critic, but doubles the time consumed by each rehearsal.

Weigh the arguments for yourself. Try rehearsal. If you find it helpful and enjoyable, then by all means continue with it. If you find that you can speak effectively without it, then don't rehearse. There is no merit in rehearsal for rehearsal's sake. The test of a speech, as we have seen, is not, "How well-rehearsed was it?" but, "Does it produce the desired effect on the audience?"

A good compromise is partial rehearsal—practicing only certain parts of the speech that are most important, or are most likely to produce difficulty.

If you elect to use this method, try rehearsing the first few and last few sentences of the speech. Also rehearse any jokes that you are going to use. Jokes, as an exception to the general rule, should be memorized. Often the omission of a single word, or its replacement by a synonym, can destroy the point of a joke. So jokes must be reproduced exactly.

Reviewing

Whether or not you rehearse all or part of your speech, you will want to review your notes several times. Look over the sheets slowly. Dwell on each idea. Think of a few phrases and sentences that you will use to express it. If you see how to make the notes clearer and more helpful, change them.

This silent review consumes less time and energy than a spoken rehearsal; nevertheless it helps to speed and facilitate the conversion of ideas into words.

Modifying the Plan

We have seen that, to obtain the desired effect, your speech must be suited to the audience. Usually you have advance information about the audience; yet you may find, when you arrive at the meeting, that the audience is not what you expected.

A snowstorm, a special program on TV, or a competitive function nearby, may give you an audience of twenty-five instead of the two hundred and fifty you had planned for. Or favorable weather and effective publicity may bring in six hundred people instead of the two hundred you were told to expect.

You may see that the audience is older or younger than you thought it would be, or that instead of a balance of the sexes, it is nearly all men or nearly all women.

To speak effectively, you will have to modify your plan. The pace that would be appropriate for two hundred and fifty people is too slow for twenty-five. To avoid falling short of your allotted time, you should add extra material. If the audience is far bigger than you expected, you will have to speak more slowly and, to avoid running over time, will need to cut some material.

Or suppose that some important event, relevant to your subject, is reported a few hours before you speak. You are to talk about crime, and on the day of the meeting the Chief-of-Police issues up-to-date crime statistics, accompanied by a projection of future trends and a plan for improved law enforcement. Your speech will be strengthened if you refer to this news.

Suppose that another speaker earlier on the program, tells an anecdote or joke that you planned to use, or treats in detail one of the points that you meant to discuss.

Suppose that, through no fault of yours, the meeting starts late, and the chairman cuts your time allotment by a quarter. Or suppose another speaker on the program fails to show up, and the chairman asks you to speak for an extra fifteen minutes.

Countless unforeseen contingencies may force you to modify your plan.

Another argument against reading a speech, memorizing and reciting it, speaking from memorized headings, or conducting frequent rehearsals is that this sets the speech in an inflexible mold, and leads to difficulties when you are forced to lengthen, abbreviate or otherwise change the speech.

Notes, on the other hand, can be changed right up to the moment when you begin to speak and, once changed, guide you smoothly through the alterations you want to make in the speech.

Here are three hints that will help you meet emergencies:

1. When planning the speech, decide which points or sections are least important and least interesting. Mark several such passages with a sign that you know means "Cut if necessary."

2. Prepare several pieces of extra material—more than you would need to fill your allotted time. Keep them on spare cards or sheets. Mark in your main notes the places where these extra items can go. "Insert Item A if needed," etc.

3. Carry a pen to make last-minute changes to your notes.

So plan the speech with care, but be prepared to modify your plan.

Summary

Whenever you can, plan your speeches.
Define your theme and write it down.
Four types of theme are:
1. To impart information
2. To inspire belief
3. To arouse emotion
4. To obtain action

Adapt your speech and delivery to suit your audience.
Cover a few points that appeal to the audience.
Make use of your own experiences and opinions.
Don't speak too long.
Notes should be brief, legible, easily handled.
Memorize jokes that form part of your speech.
Review your notes before delivering the speech.
Be ready to modify your plan.

Exercise

Here are some broad subjects:
Adult education.
The city of the future.
The housing problem.
Space travel.
Marriage and divorce laws.
The traffic problem.
Unemployment.
Forest conservation.
National parks.
Professional sports.
Liquor legislation.
Gambling.
Religion today.
The narcotics problem.
Crime and the citizen.
Newspapers in a democracy.

Criminal law reform.
Looking after your health.
Happiness for retired people.
Popular music.
The family today.
City life compared with country life.
Democracy.
Wild animals.
Present-day heroes.

Each of these subjects is too big, too vague, to be dealt with in one speech. So choose a subject, select a narrow, specific theme based upon it, and prepare a speech with a particular audience in mind.

1. 200 high-school students.
2. 25 business and professional men.
3. 50 housewives.
4. 100 retired men and women.
5. Any other kind of audience you care to define.

(See Appendix for list of more subjects)

4 .The Opening of the Speech

Great is the art of beginning.
HENRY WADSWORTH LONGFELLOW

Some speakers and textbooks refer to the first part of a speech as the introduction. To avoid confusion, we shall reserve the name "introduction" for the short speech, given by someone else to introduce a principal speaker to the audience. In this book, the first main division of a speech will be called the *opening*.

The *opening* of the speech has five functions:

1. To win the favorable attention of the audience.
2. To tell the audience what you are going to talk about.
3. To get the audience interested in the subject.
4. To unify the thoughts of the audience.
5. To set the *tone* of the speech and so unify the *emotions* of the audience.

I have numbered these functions for convenience, but they are not necessarily carried out in this order. Indeed, in a successful opening, you are usually doing two or more of them at once. Bear that in mind as we discuss them one at a time.

Win Favorable Attention

"Attention" is derived from the Latin *attendere* which means to stretch toward something. Think of a hot summer's day. You are hungry and thirsty. You are walking through a peach orchard. The owner says, "The peaches are ripe now and full of juice. Help yourself."

35

How eagerly you stretch out your hand to grasp the peach! How closely your attention is focused upon it!

This eager attention, this stretching out to grasp, to hold, to absorb, is the state you want to induce in the audience; and you want to induce it as soon as possible.

But attention is not enough—you want *favorable* attention, that is, attention accompanied by an emotional state favorable to the purpose of your speech. In other words you want the audience to trust you, to be inclined to believe what you say. You may wish to arouse admiration, respect, gratitude or affection. You certainly do not want to arouse fear, scorn, hostility, disgust or any unfavorable emotion!

Favorable attention, then, is a reaching out of the senses of sight and hearing, combined with a desirable emotional reaction toward you, the speaker.

The introduction, if you have received a good one, begins to generate favorable attention. But you cannot depend on that when planning your speech. You will not always have an introduction. When you do, the introducer may bungle his job and direct attention to himself, or to some irrelevant subject, instead of to you. A good introduction, then, is an enjoyable bonus if you get it; but always be prepared to do without it.

Even after a good introduction, the audience's attention is to some extent dissipated in the few seconds before you begin to speak. There is some wriggling, foot-shuffling and coughing as people try to get comfortable for your speech.

Your salutation, given loudly and slowly, with a sweep of your eyes over the hall, settles the audience and brings them into a state of expectancy. Now you can get off to a flying start. But if you miss the opportunity, if you create an unfavorable first impression, it may take you several minutes to recover from the setback.

Later in this chapter we shall discuss eight good opening techniques. Here let me mention two things *not* to do.

1. Don't undermine the effect of a good salutation by belittling yourself.

"I really don't know why *I* should have been asked to speak on this subject. There are fifty people in this community who know more about it than I do. But anyway. . . ."

Or, "Unfortunately I have been so busy during the past few weeks that I have had no time to prepare anything, so I'm afraid my remarks this evening will be rambling and possibly not too convincing . . .''

Or, ''I'm not what by any stretch of the imagination could be described as a speaker. Nevertheless, I'll do my poor best. Can you hear me there in the back row?''

Some speakers seem to feel that self-belittlement shows pleasing modesty. In fact, it only depresses the audience. ''Oh, dear!'' they think. ''What have we let ourselves in for now?''

Modesty is all very well in private conversation, but it is out of place on the public platform.

Do everything, by appearance, manner, voice and language, to create an impression of confidence, to radiate power to your audience, to exert the magnetic influence that will make their eyes, their thoughts and their emotions reach out toward you. To achieve this, begin *positively*.

2. Don't begin softly. Many speakers form the habit of beginning at low volume and gradually adding more power as they proceed. They call it ''warming up.''

This creates a bad impression on the audience. Some of them think, ''We won't be able to hear him!''

Even when you warm up to full power, many of them will still *think* they can't hear you, and so, in fact, will not hear you.

So don't begin softly and warm up. Begin with extra power and, if necessary, reduce volume a little as you proceed.

The cardinal fault for a speaker, the fault that cancels out every oratorical virtue, is *to be inaudible*! Resolve that, *beginning with your first sentence,* every member of the audience will hear every word you say.

Tell the Audience What You Are Going to Talk About

Tell the audience, *without delay,* what you are going to tell them. You do not, at this stage, dive right into the heart of the subject, but you do indicate clearly what that subject is.

Some speakers shrink from doing this, like swimmers afraid to jump into cold water. They ramble on about irrelevancies. Two of these delaying tactics are common enough to warrant mention.

1. *Personalities*—lengthy anecdotes about the speaker himself, or about other people who are present. There is a place for per-

sonal references in the opening, if they are kept brief. (See "Personal Reference" later in this chapter.) But there is no place for personalities that waste time and do not advance the course of the speech.

Mr. Chairman, Ladies and Gentlemen, it gives me great pleasure to be here with you tonight, especially to be on the same platform with my old teacher and friend, Professor Longfellow. It is particularly gratifying to hear, as I heard yesterday on arriving in your fair city— the city which, for so many years I called my home—it is gratifying, I say, to hear that Professor Longfellow has just published a collected edition of his works, and that that handsome edition is now on sale in the bookstores. Needless to say, my first thought was to go and purchase a set of those very handsomely-bound printed volumes. I have them here with me tonight, and after the meeting, I am going to ask Professor Longfellow to autograph them for me.

I know that when I get home and show these books to my wife— whom, by the way, I courted and married in this city, and who asks me to convey to you her deepest regrets that she is unable to be with me tonight, on account of the illness of the youngest of our two boys —as I say, when I show these books to my wife, I know she will . . . etc.

The audience is already beginning to writhe. So avoid personalities unless they bear directly on your subject.

2. *Jokes.* Some speakers feel they must begin every speech with a string of jokes. We shall discuss later the conditions under which a joke can successfully be used (they are quite limited). In most instances, the opening string of jokes has a detrimental effect. If the speaker is not highly skilled in telling jokes—and few people are—the audience is bored. If the jokes go over well, they set the thoughts of the audience wandering, and so make more difficult the task which the speaker must eventually begin, of directing those thoughts, in unison, toward the subject.

Avoid all delaying tactics. Come to the point, promptly and unmistakably, or you will lose your audience and perhaps have difficulty in recapturing them.

Here is a good example of coming to the point—the speech of the apostle Paul on Mars' Hill, in Athens (*Acts 17:22–24*).

Men of Athens, I perceive that in all things ye are too superstitious. For as I passed by and beheld your devotions, I found an altar with this inscription TO THE UNKNOWN GOD. Whom therefore ye ignorantly worship, him declare I unto you. God that made the world and all things therein. . . .

There was once a speaker who did not come to the point, and who spoke too softly. After fifteen minutes, the deaf lady in the back row said loudly to her husband, "What's he saying?"

The husband replied, "I don't know. He hasn't said yet."

Get the Audience Interested In the Subject

Interest is a feeling of *personal concern*. Imagine that each member of the audience has asked you, "Why is this subject important *to me?*" Answer that question briefly, clearly and *early,* and you immediately arouse a feeling of personal concern.

Unless this school construction referendum obtains a majority, your children are going to miss part of the education they need to earn a living and to take their place as citizens in this fast-changing society.

Such a sentence would naturally arouse the interest of an audience of parents.

It is not enough to explain why the subject is important to *you* (the speaker), or to other people, or to society at large. Each member of the audience is primarily interested in himslf, his own affairs and his own family.

Find some way to demonstrate that your subject concerns him, and you will infallibly arouse his interest.

Don't dodge this task. Don't let yourself think, "They will see for themselves that the subject is important to them. It's so obvious —it needs no comment."

You cannot be sure that *all* the audience will see it. They have not all thought about the subject as deeply as you have. Some of them may know very little about it.

Those who do already appreciate that the subject is important to them will be glad to hear you remind them of it. People like to have their own opinions confirmed by a speaker, or any other authoritative figure. That is why they tend to read newspapers whose politics coincide with their own; that is why they go to church, to have their existing beliefs strengthened.

So the answer to the question, "Why is it important to me?" will be appreciated alike by those who know it and those who do not. Give that answer confidently and clearly; it will unfailingly arouse the interest of the audience.

Unify the Thoughts of the Audience

Before the meeting begins, each member of the audience is pursuing his own line of thought. Family, work, health, neighbors, gossip, current news, movies, other people's clothes, and umpteen other things, will be on the minds and tongues of the audience.

If thoughts were visible, the audience's thoughts would be like the disorderly movement of a swarm of ants whose nest has just been broken open, all running in different directions.

It is your aim to transform that scurrying swarm into an orderly group—like a marching regiment of soldiers—and to lead them along a planned route to a predetermined destination.

So, as quickly as possible, you want to unify the thoughts of the audience, to get them thinking with you, and with each other.

This process of unification should take place naturally if you succeed in capturing attention and arousing interest. A device which will help you achieve it quickly and easily is to *begin at a point of agreement.*

As early as possible in your speech, say something that the audience must agree with—something that none of them can doubt or deny. This technique is particularly important when you face a neutral or hostile audience.

Mark Antony establishes a point of agreement when he says:

> The evil that men do lives after them;
> The good is oft interred with their bones.
> So let it be with Caesar . . .

The audience was prepared to oppose him, but he disarmed them by saying something that they had to agree with. (This speech is analyzed in Chapter 6.)

Often, in explaining why the subject is important to the listeners, you establish the point of agreement, and so unify their thoughts. Then no separate unification step is necessary. But, one way or another, it must be done, and done as soon as possible.

Set the Tone of the Speech

By the tone of a speech we mean the prevailing emotional quality. The tone may be mournful, inspiring, threatening, soothing, inflammatory, sentimental, rational, ironic, humorous, satirical, or any other you care to use.

At the start, the audience does not know how to react to the speaker, and it will seize on any clue that seems to establish the emotional relationship. So be sure not to give a false clue! *Begin* on what will be the *prevailing* emotional quality of your speech. Thus you unify the emotions of the audience.

Naturally, there will not be precise uniformity of emotion throughout the speech—it will move over a greater or smaller portion of the emotional spectrum. You can insert a touch of humor into a mainly serious speech, a few serious thoughts into a mainly light-hearted speech, and so on. The need to set the tone is another argument against beginning with a string of irrelevant jokes. If you start with humor, the audience expects you to continue with humor, and feels confused when you change to a different tone.

At the beginning of a speech, the audience is very suggestible. Take advantage of that suggestibility, and you can unify and control their emotions at will. And remember that people are moved by emotion more easily than by reason!

Nine Opening Techniques

We have examined the five functions of the opening. Now let us look at some specific ways to construct openings that will execute those functions.

1. Historical Reference

I use the adjective "historical" in a broad sense. You need not choose an incident that is recorded in books of national or world history. Simply select some bygone incident that satisfies one or more of the following conditions:

a) It must be relevant to the subject.

b) It will be more effective if it is already known to some or all of the audience.

c) It will be most effective if it is of special significance to some or all of the audience.

Suppose you are speaking at a public meeting held to discuss the possibility of increasing the water supply of your community. You could open like this:

Forty-two years ago the first public water system was constructed in this municipality, with eight hundred and seventy yards of pipe and twenty-four connections. It was ample for the needs of that time. But our present system, with its fourteen miles of pipe and three pumping stations, is not ample; it is not even adequate. Last summer, and the summer before that, you and I, Ladies and Gentlemen, had to put up with annoying restrictions on our use of water.

The special advantage of the "historical" opening is that it is a potent means of unifying the thoughts of the audience. You begin by talking about something that is established, accepted; the audience cannot help but agree with what you say. And as you win their initial agreement, you are in a good position to go on and win their agreement to whatever points you are going to make later.

(Notice also that the opening quoted above answers the questions, "What is the subject?" and "Why is it important to the listeners?")

Another example:

Fourscore and seven years ago our fathers brought forth on this continent a new nation, conceived in liberty, and dedicated to the proposition that all men are created equal.

Abraham Lincoln, when he spoke those words at Gettysburg, was well aware that he did not command the undivided support of his nation, or even of his own party. That opening was contrived to unify the thoughts of the listeners.

The "historical" opening is a useful one. An appropriate reference can be found for almost any subject and any audience.

2. Personal Reference

Open with a reference to special circumstances regarding your presence, or to your personal knowledge of the subject.

For example:

It gives me particular pleasure to speak from this platform, where my father and my grandfather spoke before me, to meetings of this same organization.

This is indisputable: the audience has no possible motive to deny or oppose the speaker. He has brought them to a point of agreement with his first sentence, and is in a favorable position to launch into his subject.

Another example:

Last November I returned to the civilized, citified part of Canada, after seven years with the Eskimos of the Northwest Territories, living as an Eskimo, eating their food, wearing their clothes, speaking their language.

The listeners cannot dispute such facts; they must follow the speaker; their thoughts are unified.

But suppose the speaker had begun like this:

A gross injustice is being inflicted on the Eskimos of the Northwest Territories by the failure of the Canadian people and the Canadian government to understand their character and their needs.

There is a risk that some of the audience would disagree, and when the listeners' thoughts are divided, instead of united, the speaker's task is more difficult.

A well-chosen personal reference, then, makes an effective opening. There are two potential dangers with this technique.

a) Don't frame the personal reference so that it sounds boastful.

b) Don't keep talking too long about yourself.

3. Quotation

Open with a quotation from an author, living or dead, or from some authority on the subject.

Omar Khayyam, the astronomer-poet of Persia, had little good to say of the wise men of the Middle East. He wrote:

> Myself when young did eagerly frequent
> Doctor and saint, and heard great argument
> About it and about, but evermore
> Came out by that same door where in I went.

Thousands of young men and women are similarly disillusioned with present-day doctors and saints: they have no respect for universities, and no reverence for churches.

Another example:

Edward Gibbon, in his *Decline and Fall of the Roman Empire,* wrote:

It has been calculated by the ablest politicians that no state, without being soon exhausted, can maintain above the hundredth part of its members in arms and idleness.

It is time, before our state becomes exhausted, to review our commitments to war and to welfare.

The quotation draws the audience into agreeing with you. In the previous example, some of them might not agree with the arithmetic, but they all must agree with your statement *that Gibbon wrote the sentence* you have quoted. You have elicited agreement on one point, have opened a crack in which to insert your wedge of evidence and argument.

4. Narrative or Description

In this opening technique, you tell a story, or draw a verbal picture.

The town of Blackboro, four hundred miles to the east of this hall, stands halfway up a mountain of coal. But the winding engines and pumps of Blackboro's four mines are standing idle. Dark water laps at the walls of the abandoned shafts. The young men have gone away from Blackboro, in search of work and money and hope. The older miners linger on, draw their unemployment pay, cultivate their rose bushes and cabbages, or sit in the Miners' Club, making one glass of beer last as long as one glass can.

The story or picture must be relevant to the subject, and it must set the correct tone for the speech that is to follow. For example, if the speaker is going to deplore the decline of coal-mining and the hardships of unemployed coal miners, it would have been inappropriate to begin the description of a riotous New Year's Eve party at the Blackboro Miners' Club.

5. Timely Reference

Open by mentioning some up-to-date fact or some recent incident.

Yesterday afternoon in the General Assembly of the United Nations, the French delegate said . . .

The National Criminal Statistics, issued last week by the Department of Justice, show that there is no pause in the frightening increase of violent crime.

This has been the coldest day of the year. I see some of you are wearing top coats and gloves. There could be no more appropriate time to discuss the need for a new heating system in our village hall.

The reference must, of course, be relevant to the subject, and appropriate in *tone* and *magnitude* to the theme of the speech. It would be absurd, for example, to describe some winter tragedy in which two hundred people froze to death as an opening for a speech on heating the village hall. Such an abrupt change of magnitude, from great to small, would produce a ludicrous effect.

6. Question

Ladies and Gentlemen, have you ever asked yourselves, "Just what am I getting in return for the dues that I pay to this organization?"

Suppose your house burned down, this evening—now, while you are sitting here—would you be covered, *fully* covered, against the loss? Do you have *all* the fire insurance you need?

As you sit here, warm, well-clothed, well-nourished, do you know how many children, right here in our city, are going to bed tonight cold, ragged and hungry?

A well-chosen, relevant question can be a powerful means of unifying the thoughts and emotions of the audience. It is particularly effective because it impels the listeners toward unity *through their own thought processes*.

There is one slight risk in asking questions of the audience, in the opening, or in any other part of your speech—the risk that someone will shout out an unwelcome answer to the question, and so disrupt the line of thought that you are following, and destroy the tone of your speech.

This will not happen with ordinary, well-behaved audiences. But if you suspect that you have troublemakers in the audience, avoid the question technique.

7. Complimentary Opening

Begin by saying something pleasant about the organization that is sponsoring the meeting, about the occasion of the meeting, or about some person or persons present.

This technique is used too often. It is acceptable on social occasions—weddings, parties, testimonial dinners, club meetings, and so on—but elsewhere it is weak and ineffective. As commonly used, it sets the wrong tone and fails either to indicate the subject of the speech, or to arouse the interest of the audience. The complimentary reference to Professor Longfellow quoted earlier in the chapter is typical.

Of course, if the purpose of the meeting is to present a gift to, or confer some honor upon, Professor Longfellow, such an opening would be appropriate.

I would suggest, then, that you use the complimentary opening sparingly, only on occasions when the purpose of your speech is to arouse feelings of goodwill. And, of course, don't use it unless you are sincere in your compliments!

8. Relevant Joke

This opening, as we have already seen, is used too often. Never open with a joke unless:

a) The joke is truly relevant to the subject.

b) You know the joke is new to the audience.

c) You can put the joke over effectively. (Remember that joke-telling is not easy.)

d) The joke will correctly set the tone of the ensuing speech.

If these conditions are fulfilled, the joke opening can be effective.

9. Bald Statement of the Subject

The subject of my remarks this evening is to be the future of trade unionism. This is a subject that is important to us all.

The subject this evening, as you have no doubt seen in the posters and newspaper advertisements, is the abolition of capital punishment. This is a very interesting and timely subject.

This opening technique is often used. Never let yourself slip into using it. It is weak and it is usually pointless, because the chairman has probably named the subject anyway.

A golden rule for the speaker is, Don't tell them the subject is interesting—*tell them something interesting about it.*

For example, instead of saying that the abolition of capital punishment is an interesting and timely subject, say, "At this moment, forty-nine murderers are sitting in the prisons of this country awaiting a date with the public executioner."

This statement is stronger; it is an interesting fact; and it forces immediate agreement.

So use the other techniques as you feel they are appropriate, but avoid the "bald statement."

Compound Opening Techniques

You need not restrict yourself to using one of the above-mentioned techniques. You can combine two or more, and so increase the power of your opening.

For example:

As a mother, I could easily get emotional over the question of capital punishment. Yesterday, here in our city, just eight blocks from this hall, a twenty-nine-year-old, one-hundred-and-eighty-pound man raped and strangled a seven-year-old girl.

This is a combination of a *personal reference* and a *timely reference*. It infallibly awakens interest and unifies the thoughts and emotions of the audience.

Consider in more detail the opening of the Gettysburg Address:

Fourscore and seven years ago our fathers brought forth on this continent a new nation, conceived in liberty, and dedicated to the proposition that all men are created equal. Now we are engaged in a great civil war, testing whether that nation, or any nation so conceived and dedicated, can long endure.

This is a combination of an *historical reference* and a *timely reference*. The question "Why is it important?" is answered by the phrases, "testing whether that nation . . . can long endure."

Open Strongly

There is a tendency among student speakers and some experienced speakers to begin with a weak first sentence, and then proceed to a second sentence which would, in fact, have made a better beginning. Here are two examples:

I want to speak this evening on the subject of juvenile delinquency. In our town, during the first eight months of this year, juvenile offenses have been running fourteen percent higher than for the same period last year.

The speaker began with a *bald statement* and went on to a *timely reference*. He would have done better to begin, "In our town, etc."

I wouldn't really call myself an expert on the subject of winemaking, but during the past few years I've made somewhat of a study of it. Winemaking—the fermentation of fruit juices to produce alcohol—was probably the first bacterial process which man learned to control.

The apologetic first sentence should have been omitted. "Wine-making—the fermentation of fruit juices, etc." is a good *historical reference,* and should have been the first sentence of the speech.

These are examples of what I call "throat-clearing openings." The speaker makes some vague, pointless noises to get himself ready for the real opening.

The habit is widespread. So check your opening to see whether, by cutting off the throat-clearing phrases, you could make it more effective.

Tell Them What You Are Going to Tell Them

At the beginning of this chapter I stated the second function of the opening—To tell the audience what you are going to talk about. This function is usually executed in the following two stages:

1. Indicate the subject of the speech.
2. Briefly specify what you are going to say about it.

In the examples cited so far I have, for simplicity's sake, stopped at stage 1. But the opening is not complete until stage 2 has also been effected. Let us see how, in some instances, this could be done.

Consider the first example of the *historical reference opening.*

Forty-two years ago the first public water system was constructed in this municipality, with eight hundred and seventy yards of pipe and twenty-four connections. It was ample for the needs of that time. But our present system, with its fourteen miles of pipe and three pumping stations, is *not* ample; it is not even adequate. Last summer, and the summer before that, you and I, Ladies and Gentlemen, had to put up with annoying restrictions on our use of water.

But I am going to lay before you a scheme that will put an end to water restrictions, that within eighteen months will give us an ample water supply. Your water board has located three never-failing springs of pure water, which can easily and cheaply be tapped. We can secure, on favorable terms, a right of way for the necessary pipeline. We already own the site for a new pumping station and reservoir.

And, by a very moderate increase in the water rate, we can bring to each home in the municipality the water we need for comfortable, convenient, healthy living.

Now, the biggest of the three springs is located . . .

The opening ends with the words ". . . healthy living." With the next sentence, "Now, the biggest of the three springs . . ." the speaker moves into the *body* of the speech. There he will develop in detail the points that he mentioned briefly in the opening.

Here is another example, one of those cited under category 3, *Quotation*:

Omar Khayyam, the astronomer-poet of Persia, had little good to say of the wise men of the Middle East. He wrote:

> Myself when young did eagerly frequent
> Doctor and saint, and heard great argument
> About it and about, but evermore
> Came out by that same door where in I went.

Thousands of young men and women are similarly disillusioned with present-day doctors and saints: they have no respect for universities, and no reverence for churches.

Why do young people feel like this? Let us look at our educational and religious systems, and try to find an answer.

Are the right people going to our universities? How many potentially capable students are excluded for one reason or another? Of those who do attend, how many are wasting their own time and the public's money?

How meaningful is the university curriculum to boys and girls growing up in the age of the computer, the heart transplant and the hydrogen bomb?

Who are the teachers? How are they recruited? How competent are they? Are they fit to lead, to inspire, to win the respect of the students of today?

And what about the churches? What do they say to young adults? Is their message revolutionary or conservative?

And church government: to what extent are young people given a voice? Or are the churches ruled by old people? And if so, why?

In examining these questions, we may find some ideas that will enable us better to understand the attitudes of young people; we may be able to help those young people find a more satisfying role in society.

So who goes, and who doesn't go, to university? . . .

Here, the sentence ending ". . . role in society." finishes the opening. "So, who goes. . . ." begins the body of the speech. We see the same useful opening format: a brief preview of the ground to be covered.

The Length of the Opening

I suggested in Chapter 2 that the opening should be about one-tenth of the speech. Naturally, the shorter the total length of the speech, the fewer points you can cover in the body of it, so the less preparatory material you will need in the opening. A longer speech, with more points discussed (or with the same number of points more fully discussed) in the body, will require more preparation with a longer opening.

The "water supply" opening given above would serve for a speech of about twelve to fifteen minutes, depending on the speaker's rate of delivery.

The "Omar Khayyam" opening would be appropriate for a speech of about eighteen to twenty-five minutes.

There is no iron-bound rule that says the opening must be one-tenth of the whole, but this will be a useful guide for planning your early speeches.

Summary

Functions of the opening:
1. To win favorable attention.
2. To indicate your subject.
3. To arouse interest in the subject.
4. To unify the thoughts of the audience.
5. To unify the emotions of the audience.

Don't begin with apologies or self-belittlement.

Begin loudly, begin strongly.

Announce your subject promptly.

Indicate what you are going to say about it.

Arouse in the audience a sense of personal concern.

Begin at a point of agreement.

Begin on the prevailing emotional tone of the speech.

The Nine Opening techniques are:

1. Historical reference
2. Personal reference
3. Quotation
4. Narrative or description
5. Timely reference
6. Question
7. Complimentary opening
8. Relevant joke
9. Bald statement of subject (Not recommended)

Where possible, use compound opening techniques.

Let your opening be about one-tenth of your speech.

Exercise

Take a subject from the list following Chapter 3. Choose a theme based upon it. Construct three different openings for a speech on that theme.

5. The Body of the Speech

Prove all things.

I Thessalonians, 1:3

If you have properly prepared and delivered the opening, your audience—with interest awakened and thoughts unified—will be eager to follow you into the body of the speech.

The opening served, among other functions, to "tell them what you are going to tell them"; now, in the body, it is time to "tell them."

What are you to tell them, and how? As we saw in Chapter 3, it is seldom possible in one speech to cover the whole of a subject: the best plan is to deal with *a few points only*—points chosen for their interest and helpfulness to the audience. For most speeches, five main points will be enough.

Selecting the Points

I suggested that the most interesting and helpful points should be chosen. We have defined interest as a feeling of personal concern. With some subjects and themes, you will have little difficulty in leading the audience toward this personal concern. For example, any speech that touches on such things as taxes, health, work, education or housing will personally concern most members of the average audience. They know at once that such things concern them.

But with some themes—particularly those of Type 1, which seek to impart information—the audience may not voluntarily and quickly come to feel this personal concern. "The Sculpture of

Michelangelo,'' for example. How does that personally concern the average present-day city dweller? How can you get him concerned with the Emperor Constantine or Napoleon Bonaparte, with the discovery of the planet Neptune, the bacterial contamination of the water in a nearby river, the nesting habits of the bald eagle, or the techniques of manufacturing paper towels?

The best way to arouse interest in any subject is to borrow a technique used by fiction writers; that is, depict a *conflict* of some kind. Conflict tends to arouse a reader's interest, and it will similarly tend to arouse a listener's interest.

If you are talking about ''The Sculpture of Michelangelo,'' for example, a mere listing and description of the artist's major statues would probably be dull. But if you talk about his struggles to master his art, the cost of his materials and his sometimes stormy relationships with his patrons, your speech will acquire considerable interest.

Merely to name the bacteria that are found in river water might be dull. But if you say how sunshine, aeration and temperature changes affect the bacterial population, you are describing a life-and-death conflict in the microscopic world, and that is interesting. If you describe how the water supply authority is constantly struggling to reduce the bacterial contamination, while domestic and industrial effluents continually tend to increase it, you have an interesting conflict.

Conflict interests listeners because they themselves are constantly in conflict with family, friends and employers, with society and its laws and regulations (breaking speed limits, paying taxes, criticizing the government), with nature (heat, cold, mosquitoes, sickness, death) and with themselves (striving against laziness, overweight, alcohol, bad temper).

Therefore, as you portray a conflict, whether it is between Michelangelo and Pope Julius II between bald eagles and hunters, between Napoleon and his schoolmasters, or between the inherent flimsiness of paper and an inventor's desire to make it tough and water resistant—the listener can, to some extent, identify himself with it. ''Yes, that's something like the problem that I have with so-and-so.''

Now we come to some specific hints on selecting the points to be used in a speech.

1. Write down all the points you can think of. A few words will do for each.

2. Choose for your speech at least one point that contains a strong element of conflict.

3. Choose, if you can find it, a point that will help listeners to understand or resolve some conflict or problem of their own.

4. Choose enough additional points to fill out the required length of your speech, preferably taking other points with an element of conflict, or of help for the listener.

As an example, let us look at the speech on "Methods of Delivering a Speech" that we discussed in Chapter 2.

Point 1: Reading. Here the would-be speaker is in conflict with himself. He is afraid that he will not know what to say, yet he wants to deliver the speech as effectively as possible. He is advised that reading is not an effective method of delivery.

Point 2: Recitation. Here is more conflict, between the speaker's wish to be word-perfect, and his natural reluctance to spend a long time memorizing.

Point 3: Memorized Headings. This is another conflict between the desire to have a well-arranged speech, and the fear of forgetting the headings, which would result in a disorganized speech.

Point 4: Notes. The conflict is resolved, with the least amount of work, the least strain on the memory, and the best results. The listener is offered practical help.

In any speech, then, points which depict conflict tend to be interesting; points which resolve conflict for the listener tend to be helpful. (Helpful points are interesting, too, of course.) A point which depicts no conflict, and is not helpful, tends to be dull.

Arranging the Points

Effective arrangement of the points of your speech can do much to help the audience understand and accept what you say; clumsy arrangement of the same material can leave the audience uninformed or skeptical. Here are some useful arrangements.

1. Arrangement by Space

With some subjects, it is natural to deal with the various points in the same order in which they are arranged in space. For example, a speech on "A Visit to an Art Exhibition" could discuss the exhibits in the order that the visitor saw them in walking through the gallery.

A speech on "How to Judge Beef Cattle" could describe the good and bad points of a typical animal, beginning at the head and ending with the tail.

The description of a geographical region could cover the area from north to south, from coast to mountains, from source to mouth of the principal river, or in some other coherent spatial order.

The listener will easily follow such orderly treatment; but he will be confused if you dart hither and thither over the ground covered by your subject.

2. Arrangement by Time

For historical subjects, for biographies and for personal narratives, this arrangement works well. It would be natural in speaking about a man's career to begin with his training and end with his retirement.

Time-order is appropriate for many technical subjects, too. For example, in talking about gardening, you could arrange your points by time, because success depends on performing the various operations—digging, sowing, transplanting, watering, harvesting, etc.—at the right time.

A speech on "Producing a Stage Play" would naturally describe all the preparations, rehearsals and performances in order of time.

Whenever there is an obvious time-order connected with the subject, you may as well make use of it in arranging the points of your speech.

3. Cause-and-Effect Arrangement

For a speech on "How I Stopped Smoking" the time-arrangement might be suitable. But to cover the general question of "Smoking and Health" the cause-and-effect arrangement would probably be more effective.

"Air Pollution and Respiratory Disease," "Pesticides and

Bird Population," "Alcohol and Traffic Accidents"—in such subjects there is an obvious cause-and-effect relationship; so build your speech on that relationship.

You can begin with describing the causes (or all the causes you have time for) and end by describing their effects. Alternatively, you can begin by describing the effect and then go on to reveal and discuss its causes.

To decide which treatment to use, consider what the audience knows about the subject, and follow the general rule: *Begin with what they know and lead on to what they don't know.*

For example, suppose you are talking about "The Traffic Problem." Everyone knows about traffic jams, collisions, injuries and deaths on the road (that is *the effect*). So begin by vividly describing the effect, then go on to discuss its causes.

But suppose you are to speak on "Noise and Health," showing how noise tends to produce certain mental and physical ailments. Everyone is familiar with noise (that is *the cause*). So begin with the cause and then proceed to describe what is less familiar, its effect.

4. Problem-Solution Arrangement

"Methods of Delivering a Speech" was a problem-solution arrangement. "Efficient Job Application Methods," "Physiotherapy for Hand and Arm Injuries," "Safety Measures for Swimming and Boating"—these are typical subjects that could be dealt with by the problem-solution arrangement.

State the problem first, using as many points as are necessary to cover its major aspects, then describe the possible solutions.

5. Analytical Arrangement

For some themes and subjects, the points do not fall into any obvious order of space, time, cause-effect or problem-solution. "What Democracy Means to Me," "My Favorite Song," "Should Capital Punishment Be Abolished?"—with such subjects you simply have to select the points you will make, and then try to arrange them to best effect.

If some of the material is new to the audience, begin with what they know, and lead on to what is unfamiliar. If all the material is equally familiar to the audience, arrange the points as follows: the most interesting point should come last (immediately before the conclusion); the second most interesting point should come first (immediately after the opening) and the others, of less interest, should come in between.

6. Combined Arrangements

You may sometimes need to combine two of these schemes. For example, if the subject is not too big in scope, you might be able to deal with cause-effect and problem-solution in one speech. That would probably be too much to attempt with big subjects like "Alcoholism," "Violent Crime" or "Water Pollution."

But you could do it with simpler subjects such as "Patchy Growth in Lawns," "Unpunctuality" or "Memory Training." In each case, you would deal first with causes, next with effects. The effect (bare patches on the lawn, tardiness, forgetfulness) is a problem, so you could then discuss means of solving it.

Arrangement Essential

You may devise other methods of arranging the points in the body of your speech. It does not matter what you call your arrangement; the important thing is that there should be a system of some kind. The events of everyday life often seem disorganized; they follow each other without any reasonable connection. That will not do for a speech; the audience expects a speech to be *more orderly, more comprehensible,* than life. Life often leaves people puzzled; a good speech leaves them enlightened. A systematic arrangement of your material makes an important contribution to that enlightenment.

Treatment of the Points

The formula for treating each point is:
    1. State it.

2. Demonstrate it.

3. Recapitulate it.

Let us examine each stage separately.

1. State It

Stage 1 is easy—simply state in plain words the point that you are about to make.

The first sentence that follows the opening will naturally be the statement of the first point of the body. Look back at the two examples toward the the end of Chapter 4.

"Now the biggest of the three springs . . ." obviously indicates the subject of the speaker's first point.

"So, who goes, and who doesn't go, to university?" is the statement of the first point.

Here are the points from a speech of mine about "Trade Unionism and Social Change." Following the opening, I said:

There has been a steady, general increase of wealth among the workers. Let's look at the causes and the extent of that increased wealth, and let's see how trade unions are adjusting to it.

That was the statement of my first point. Then I proceeded to demonstrate it.

The second point:

It's fair to say that this is now becoming a nation of capitalists. More and more ordinary citizens are buying and holding the common stock of the nation's industries. What effect will this development have on unions and unionism?

The third point:

Now let's look at a subject particularly important to trade unions: the growth of moonlighting—the ever-increasing number of men and women who hold two jobs. One of those jobs may be a regular, unionized job by day, but the other, in the evenings or at weekends, is likely to be non-unionized. How does this affect the moonlighter's loyalty to the union movement?

The fourth point:

Another great social change is the steady increase of state welfare activities. Government is taking over the trade unions' old role as champion of the working man. Is this weakening the influence of the unions?

The fifth point:

There are vast, continuing changes in the makeup of the labor force, and there are constant changes in the nature of the work available for the labor force. The trade unions are not keeping abreast of these changes.

So state each point clearly before you begin to demonstrate it; then the audience knows exactly what aspect of the subject you are talking about at any moment.

Unmistakable statement of your points is a great step toward clarity. Remember the deaf lady in the back row. *You cannot be too clear.*

2. Demonstrate It

When you have stated your point, demonstrate it, so that the audience will agree with you, and admit the point. Or, if the audience already believes the truth of the point, demonstrate it to reinforce their belief.

Moreover, and not less important, the demonstration helps the audience to *remember* the point. If you were to state the point and quickly pass on, most listeners would forget it. But if you talk about it at length, refute criticisms of it, give examples of it, and hold it pleasantly and interestingly in the minds of the audience for several minutes, you have made sure that some of them, at least, will not forget it.

Here are six methods of demonstrating a point:

    (1) Appeal to reason
    (2) Cite examples
    (3) Quote statistics
    (4) Quote an authority
    (5) Draw a comparison
    (6) Appeal to emotion

Let us examine these methods one at a time and see the advantages and disadvantages of each.

Appeal to Reason

Suppose your point is that people should not gamble on sweepstakes. You could appeal to reason by saying something like this:

It is unwise to spend money on sweepstake tickets because the odds are fifty thousand to one against your winning a worthwhile prize. A prudent, sensible man would not make such a dubious investment. It is more reasonable to put your money in a bank, where you can have it again at any time, and meanwhile draw five percent interest on it.

Do you think that such an appeal to reason would stop anyone from buying sweepstake tickets?

Or suppose your point was that drinking hard liquor is a bad habit, and you said:

It is obvious that the mouth exists for the purpose of taking in nourishment. Therefore it is unreasonable to take into the mouth anything that is going to harm the body. Excessive consumption of hard liquor has been proven to undermine health. Therefore the reasonable man will not drink hard liquor.

A teetotaler would agree with you, of course, but would such a demonstration have any power to influence the regular liquor-drinker?

Or suppose you were campaigning for public office.

Friends, I have an intelligence quotient of one hundred and fifty. My own life is smoothly organized and happy. My own business runs like clockwork; my employees are prosperous and contented. Is it not reasonable that a man who has shown his ability to look after his own business should be entrusted with part of the public's business?

This is all perfectly reasonable, perfectly true, but I doubt it would win many votes.

The appeal to reason is not generally effective with an audience. Most people do *not* reason their way through life. They do not respond readily to reasonable arguments. They tend to get annoyed with the man who insists upon reasoning with them. Perhaps this is because the appeal to reason seems to imply superiority on the part of the speaker: "Now, listen, you people, and I'll explain the problem to you the way that a thinking man sees it, etc."

An appeal to reason should not be made the main support of any point. It can be used as a supplement when the point has already been established by other means.

Cite Examples

State your point and then cite one or more examples of it. Here is a point from a speech of mine on "The Development of Poetry:"

Shakespeare thought highly of his own poetry: he knew it was good, and he was confident that it would live. But he certainly did not think he was the best poet of his day. He often admitted that other writers outshone him.

Then follow examples:

For instance, in Sonnet 79 he writes:

But now my gracious numbers are decayed
And my sick Muse doth give another place.

In Sonnet 80 he returns to the idea of a better poet who has ousted him from favor:

O, how I faint when I of you do write,
Knowing a better spirit doth use your name . . .
My saucy bark inferior far to his
On your broad main doth wilfully appear . . .

And again, in Sonnet 85:

My tongue-tied Muse in manners holds her still,
While comments of your praise, richly compiled,
Reserve their character with golden quill
And precious phrase by all the Muses filed.
I think good thoughts while others write good words . . .

Suppose your point is: "Violent crime is increasing in our city." You can demonstrate it by recounting several violent crimes that have occurred recently.

Or suppose you want to demonstrate the point: "Weight-control makes you feel healthy." A personal example would be good: tell how you reduced weight, and describe how much better you feel as a result.

Or suppose your point is: "Mr. X has served this city well as Mayor." It is natural to demonstrate the point by citing examples of the wise, popular things X has done during his term of office.

This technique is a strong one—so convincing that it is used in courts of law to establish or belittle the reputation of a witness. There is a natural feeling that, if you cite examples of a man's honorable, upright conduct on other occasions, he is probably being honorable and upright now; examples of previous dishonesty tend to undermine his credibility in the present.

So search for good examples of the points you wish to demonstrate. Use them freely. They tend to make your speech interesting and convincing.

Quote Statistics

When you quote statistics to demonstrate a point you are in effect citing a large number of examples.

Suppose a present-day speaker was demonstrating Franklin's point: "Most men, as well as most sects in religion, think themselves in possession of the truth, etc."

He might continue: "A survey of public attitudes toward religion, conducted in this city last year, showed that sixty-six percent of regular church-goers believe their sect is the only one that offers a true religion."

This is an effective use of statistics. Many interviews presumably have been conducted, and their significance has been distilled down to a few conveniently quotable figures.

But don't quote too many statistics! Suppose you want to demonstrate the point: "A major cause of the population explosion is the increase of the average life-span."

Then suppose you continued: "In the United States, in 1900,

the average life-span was 47.3 years; in 1961 it was 70.2 years. In Canada, from 1931 to 1961, the male life expectancy at birth rose from 60 years to 68.35 years; the female life expectancy at birth rose from 62.1 years to 74.17 years.''

This is too much of a good thing. The audience could not absorb so many figures thrown at them so fast. Numerical information is not as easy to grasp when you hear it spoken as when you read it on the printed page. When you read figures in a book, you can dwell on them, think what they mean and look them over again if need be. Your audience cannot do this!

So, to sum up, statistics are useful in demonstration, but *use them sparingly.*

Quote an Authority

To demonstrate a point you can quote a statement by someone who may be supposed to know more about the subject than do you or your listeners.

For example, to show that ''Kindergarten schools are important'' you could quote Plato: ''The direction in which education starts a man will determine his future life.''

Or to demonstrate that ''Political apathy endangers democracy'' you could cite Jean Jacques Rousseau: ''As soon as public service ceases to be the chief business of the citizens, and they would rather serve with their money than with their persons, the State is not far from its fall.''

Or suppose you want to demonstrate the point: ''Welfare-statism is not true democracy.'' You could cite Grover Cleveland: ''The lessons of paternalism ought to be unlearned and the better lesson taught that while the people should patriotically and cheerfully support their government, its functions do not include the support of the people.''

The quotation from an authority, if well chosen, carries great weight with an audience. It is third-party testimony—not what you, the speaker, say about the subject, but what some independent person has said about it.

You can find suitable material in a dictionary of quotations arranged or indexed by subjects. For up-to-date quotations, watch your newspaper. Clip out authoritative statements concerning subjects that you are likely to be speaking about.

Draw a Comparison

A powerful means of demonstrating a point is to draw a comparison. You explain something that is new to the audience by saying that *it is like* something familiar.

See how Abraham Lincoln used a comparison to demonstrate the rather difficult point that liberty means different things to different people:

We all declare for liberty, but in using the same word we do not at all mean the same thing. The shepherd drives the wolf from the sheep's throat, for which the sheep thanks him as his liberator, while the wolf denounces him for the same act, as the destroyer of liberty. Plainly the sheep and the wolf are not agreed upon a definition of the word 'Liberty'.

Socrates used the same method. "Public officials ought not to be chosen by lot" is his point. He demonstrated it by drawing two comparisons. "That is like drawing lots to select athletes, instead of choosing those who are fit for the competition; that is like drawing lots among a ship's crew to select a helmsman, instead of choosing the man who best knows how to steer."

Read the fables of Aesop and the parables of Jesus of Nazareth; you will find them excellent examples of demonstration by comparison.

It is usually easy to find a comparison for any point that you want to demonstrate. Simply ask yourself, *"What is it like?"* Tell the audience *what it is like*, and they will have a better idea of *what it is*.

Appeal to Emotion

To appeal to the listeners' emotion is the most effective (and potentially the most dangerous) method of getting them to accept your point. It is such a big subject that it needs a chapter to itself (see Chapter 6).

3. Recapitulate It

When you have finished demonstrating, recapitulate the point. Possibly some of the audience did not grasp it the first time it was stated. During the demonstration, they have gradually been getting hold of the idea. Now they want to hear it summed up briefly and forcefully.

If you want to express the point in different words, that is acceptable; if you want to repeat it in its original form, there is no harm in that.

If the original statement of the point included a question, then it is appropriate for the recapitulation to be framed as the answer to the question.

For example, take the point that I quoted earlier, from the speech about ''Trade Unionism and Social Change.'' The original statement of the point was:

Now let's look at a subject particularly important to trade unions: the growth of moonlighting—the ever-increasing number of men and women who hold two jobs. One of those jobs may be a regular, unionized job by day, but the other, in the evenings, or at weekends, is likely to be non-unionized. How does this affect the moonlighter's loyalty to the union movement?

I demonstrated this point in five steps.
1) Cited examples to show the causes of moonlighting.
2) Quoted an authority (a union leader) on the unions' hatred and fear of moonlighters.
3) Appealed to reason showing second job reduces dependence on union.
4) Quoted authorities (other union leaders) showing work-week gets shorter still.
5) Appealed to reason showing that this will increase moonlighting.

Then came the recapitulation:

So moonlighting, as it now exists, is seen by the trade unions as a threat. Yet the progressive shortening of the work week can only mean that more workers will be moonlighting for more hours, and making more of their income from non-unionized employment. This increased moonlighting must reduce the dependence of the workers on their trade unions.

You can help considerably to maintain the interest of the audience if you use the recapitulations to keep reminding them that each aspect of the subject is important to them. The speech from which the previous example is taken was delivered to an audience of trade-unionists, so the recapitulation clearly implied, ''Moonlighting is important to you, as workers and as trade-unionists.''

Mark off the Points

Your speech should not be a smooth, non-stop flow of words. Don't glide without a break from one point to the next. After recapitulating each point, be sure the audience knows you are finished with it. Look down at your notes; make a long pause. The listener then feels, ''He's said all he's going to say about that point. Now I can prepare myself to hear something different.''

After the long pause and the downward look, raise your head briskly, and begin speaking at a different pitch, a different pace, and a different power. This strong vocal change has a stimulating effect on the audience. It tends to enliven them and make them more eager to hear your next point.

But never mark off your points with an apology.

I've perhaps been talking too long about moonlighting, so let's move on to something else.

At the risk of overstepping your patience, I will now take up the question of . . .

Summary

For the body, select a few interesting, helpful points.
Interest can be aroused by depicting conflict.
Five arrangements of the points:
1. By space
2. By time
3. Cause-and-effect
4. Problem-solution
5. Analytical
Treatment of each point: *state, demonstrate, recapitulate.*
Six ways to demonstrate a point:
1. Appeal to reason (Weak if used alone)
2. Cite examples (Strong)

3. Quote statistics (Strong, but use sparingly)
4. Quote an authority (Strong)
5. Draw a comparison (Strong)
6. Appeal to emotion (Strongest)

Mark off a new point by pause and vocal change.

Exercises

1. Take three different subjects and for each subject select five points that would be appropriate:
   a) To an audience of high-school students.
   b) To an audience of university students.
   c) To an audience of adults, most of whom have children in school.
   d) To an audience of people retired from work.
   e) To an audience of trade-union members.
   f) To an audience of people living in a small village.
   g) To an audience of big-city dwellers.
   h) To an audience of immigrants who have not yet received citizenship.

2. Take the sets of points selected above and arrange them in the order that would be most effective for each audience.

3. Take one of the speech outlines you have thus prepared, and plan an opening for it.

4. For the same speech outline, write down the means you would use to demonstrate each of the points.

6. Appeal to Emotion

Men are so made that they can resist sound argument, and yet yield to a glance.
HONORÉ DE BALZAC

We saw in Chapter 5 that the body of a speech consists of a small number of points, chosen because they are relevant to the subject and interesting to the audience. You state each of these points in turn, then demonstrate it—that is, use rhetorical techniques that tend to make listeners understand your statement, believe it, remember it and, if necessary, act upon it. The sixth of those techniques, the appeal to emotion, is the subject of this chapter.

Aristotle, in his "Rhetoric," said that the appeal to emotion is important because it is *quicker* and *more certain* than an appeal to reason. (If I were making a speech, this would be "quoting an authority.")

We already have seen that many people are not guided at all by reason. Similarly some people may not be impressed by an example ("One swallow doesn't make a summer"), may distrust statistics, dispute the word of an authority, or be blind to the meaning of a comparison. But everyone can be moved by emotion.

Some beginning speakers feel embarrassed at appealing to emotion, as if it were ill-mannered or discreditable. They feel that way because they do not make emotional appeals in ordinary polite conversation. To be sure, in moments of crisis, talking to people you know well, you do appeal to their emotions: "You'd do it if you really loved me!" or "For heaven's sake, aren't you ashamed of yourself?" etc.

But such appeals are usually made in private. In our society, general conversation tends to be somewhat unemotional, except for displays of mirth.

But public speaking is not conversation! Methods that are adequate for conversation fail in public speaking. Methods that would seem absurd in the living room seem natural, and are highly effective, on the platform. So don't be afraid to appeal to emotion.

Neither is there anything immoral about appealing to the emotions of your audience. Morality or immorality lies in the purpose of your speech, not in the techniques you use to deliver it. If your purpose is worthy—to inform, to help, to inspire your listeners—then you will naturally want to use the most effective means of fulfilling that purpose.

Basic Emotions

An emotion is an excited state of mind, either pleasant or unpleasant. There are countless shades in the emotional spectrum, but for practical purposes we can classify the useful emotions under ten headings, consisting of five approximately opposite pairs.

1. Love
2. Hatred
3. Mirth
4. Grief
5. Pride
6. Shame
7. Hope
8. Fear
9. Desire
10. Contentment

Let us examine these emotions, see what each one consists of, how it can be aroused, and how it may serve the speaker.

1. Love

Love may be directed toward parents, husband, wife or children. Here is an example of an appeal to love.

You naturally want your children to get the very best possible education, an education that will fit them to grow up and take their places as happy, prosperous citizens. That first-class education can be theirs, Ladies and Gentlemen, if you support the forthcoming school finance referendum. So I urge you . . . . etc.

Love of the Deity is the basis of religion, and religious appeals are used—though not so often as they used to be—by speakers. There can be a generalized love (philanthropy or benevolence) that extends to people the audience has never seen or known.

Friends, I present to you the case of a pair of twin girls, aged eight, both eager to go to school, to learn, to salvage something from their ruined lives in that ruined land. But they have only one ragged little dress between the two of them. So, while one is at school, the other stays hiding in the shack they call a home. They take it in turns to stay home, and each evening the one who has been to school tries to pass on to her sister the lesson she has learned. Friends, those of you who have closets half full of unworn clothing, I appeal to you, etc.

There is love for someone who has done something praiseworthy —we call it admiration.

There is the love of one who has conferred benefits on us—we call it gratitude.

There is even love for the person who has injured us—we call it forgiveness. It can sometimes be aroused, and used to good effect by the speaker.

2. Hatred

You may feel hatred for personal enemies who have injured or tried to injure you. You may hate the enemies of your country.

Hatred finds expression in insult, contempt, ridicule and satire. Hatred inspires feelings of indignation and anger; it inspires a craving for revenge.

Here is an extract from a speech by William Pitt the Younger, in which he seeks to stir up hatred and scorn against the revolutionary government of France.

All the crimes which disgrace history have occurred in one country, in a space so short, and with circumstances so highly aggravated, as outrun thought and exceed imagination. Should we treat with Marat, before we had finished the negotiation he might again have descended to the dregs of the people from whom he sprang and have given place to a still more desperate villain.

Pitt arouses this emotion to help attain his aim, to persuade his listeners to have no dealings with the revolutionaries.

Here is part of the speech delivered by Richard Brinsley Sheridan at the trial of Warren Hastings (1732–1818) for corruption and cruelty in his administration of India. Edmund Burke, himself a brilliant orator, said that this speech of Sheridan's was "the most astonishing effort of eloquence of which there is any record or tradition."

Middleton was appointed, in 1777, the confidential agent, the second self, of Mr. Hastings. The Governor-General [i.e., Hastings] ordered the measure. Even if he never saw nor heard afterwards of its consequences, he was therefore answerable for every pang that was inflicted, and for all the blood that was shed. But he did hear, and that instantly, of the whole. He wrote to accuse Middleton of forbearance and of neglect! He commanded him to work on the hopes and fears of the princesses, and to leave no means untried until, to speak his own language, which was better suited to the banditti of a cavern, "he obtained possession of the secret hoards of the old ladies."

He would not allow even of a delay of two days to smooth the compelled approaches of a son to his mother on this occasion! His orders were peremptory.

After this, my lords, can it be said that the prisoner was ignorant of the acts, or not culpable for their consequences? It is true he did not direct the guards, the famine and the bludgeons; he did not weigh the fetters, nor number the lashes to be inflicted on his victims; but yet he is just as guilty as if he had borne an active and personal share in each transaction. It is as if he had commanded that the heart should be torn from the bosom, and enjoined that no blood should follow. He is in the same degree accountable to the law, to his country, to his conscience, and to his God!

This effectively stirs up hatred and scorn for the accused. Of course, the speech of an advocate is not evidence, but it often happens in courts of law that if an advocate succeeds in making the jurors hate the prisoner, then they will tend to feel that he must be guilty. Similarly, if the advocate for the defense can make the jurors like the prisoner, they will tend to feel that he must be innocent.

The same principle applies in platform speaking. The more effectively you can arouse the emotions of your audience, the stronger becomes your power to persuade them.

3. Mirth

Mirth, of all the ten emotions, is most likely to produce an audible reaction from the audience—laughter. Millions of adults who would be ashamed to sob with grief or howl with rage in public will gladly roar with mirth in sight of their fellow-citizens.

The audience that experiences mirth tends to generate a favorable feeling toward the speaker *and toward the subject*. This is not a conscious reaction. The listener does not deliberately think, "Such-and-such a subject has given me some laughs, therefore it is interesting, and I will follow it up, and do what the speaker says."

No, the listener reacts unconsciously to the mirth that the speaker has consciously aroused.

Mirth is the audience's reaction to humor and wit. But humor and wit are double-edged tools, and should be used with certain precautions.

Humorous material must be relevant to the theme. Irrelevant jokes, to be sure, can arouse mirth, but then the listener will become favorably disposed toward the subject of the jokes. He will feel disappointed—even resentful—when you eventually drag him away from the jokes and try to direct his attention to the subject and theme of your speech.

Relevant humor and wit, then, will help, and irrelevant humor and wit will hinder, your efforts to persuade and to move the audience.

The field for successful humor continually grows more restricted. At one time a speaker could crack jokes about deafness and blindness, about Negroes and Irishmen, about Jews and Baptist preachers, about the supposed stupidity of foreigners, and so on. We have grown, and are continually growing, more sensitive, more tactful. Such subjects are already taboo with intelligent speakers and audiences. New taboos are being erected all the time.

One fairly safe subject for mirth, of course, is yourself. Raise a laugh against yourself, and few people will be annoyed with you.

There are books of jokes and witticisms, specially prepared for speakers, with entries classified by subjects. Newspapers and magazines continually print up-to-date humorous stories and quips on all kinds of subjects. If you wish to use humor in your speeches, begin to build a file of suitable material.

Study how experienced speakers work to rouse mirth in their audiences. Don't try too soon to make the appeal to mirth. It is one of the hardest branches of the speaker's art. Wait until you feel you can do it easily, naturally, and with perfect confidence.

Another point is to let your use of this appeal be consistent with your character and general speaking technique. If you are a jolly, hearty kind of person; if you tend to speak with a high degree of emotion, and to laugh loudly yourself; then work toward the use of a loud, hearty kind of humor in your speeches, and aim to get the audience roaring with laughter.

But if you are a restrained, thoughtful speaker, let your humor be in tone with your character and technique; aim for chuckles rather than belly laughs.

Detailed hints on the way to deal with a laughing audience are given in Chapter 19.

Here is an example of the use of humor, from a speech by Benjamin Franklin. His point was, ''Most men, as well as most sects in religion, think themselves in posession of all truth, and that wherever others differ from them, it is so from error.''

Then he gives two humorous examples.

Steele, a Protestant, in a dedication, tells the Pope that the only difference between our two churches in their opinions of the certainty of their doctrines is, the Romish Church is infallible, and the Church of England is never in the wrong.

But, though many private persons think almost as highly of their own infallibility as of that of their sect, few express it so naturally as a certain French lady who, in a dispute with her sister, said: ''But I meet with nobody but myself that is always in the right!''

Franklin's first anecdote would be a risky one to use nowadays. The second would probably be acceptable.

4. Grief

Abraham Lincoln made an appeal to grief in his Gettysburg Address. It was appropriate to the occasion which was the dedication of a war cemetery.

. . . . But, in a larger sense, we cannot dedicate—we cannot consecrate—we cannot hallow—this ground. The brave men, living and dead, who struggled here, have consecrated it far above our poor power to add or detract. The world will little note nor long remember what we say here, but it can never forget what they did here. It is for us, the living, rather to be dedicated here to the unfinished work which they who fought here have thus so nobly advanced . . . .

Having aroused the emotion of grief, he goes on to urge his theme, the need for vigorous prosecution of the war. He implies, "You share my grief—we are agreed on that—so share my plans, and my determination to execute them."

This is a typical example of the effect of an emotional appeal— people who *share an emotional experience* tend to feel closer, better disposed toward each other. For example, people who share fear—say in an earthquake, fire or war—will temporarily forget their habitual reserve. They will talk to strangers, smile at them, help them, open their homes to them, give them food and clothing. But, as the emotion passes away, so does its effect; the barriers are raised again.

So the speaker takes advantage of the *temporary susceptibility caused by shared emotion*—takes advantage of it to implant his ideas, to inspire belief or to suggest action.

5. Pride

Pride is a feeling of satisfaction in one's own good qualities or accomplishments. It is closely allied with courage. The proud man will not let anyone see him turn tail; he puts on a bold front and advances toward the thing that he fears.

Shakespeare gives Henry V an appeal to pride before the battle of Agincourt *(Henry V, Act IV, Sc. 3)*:

This day is called the feast of Crispian:
He that outlives this day, and comes safe home
Will stand a tip-toe when the day is named
And rouse him at the name of Crispian.
He that shall live this day, and see old age,
Will yearly on this vigil feast his neighbors,
And say, "Tomorrow is Saint Crispian"
Then will he strip his sleeve and show his scars,
And say, "These wounds I had on Crispian's day."
Old men forget: yet all shall be forgot,
But he'll remember with advantages
What feats he did that day. . . . . . .
And gentlemen in England now abed
Shall think themselves accursed they were not here,
And hold their manhoods cheap while any speaks
That fought with us upon Saint Crispian's day.

Patrick Henry appealed to pride when he said:

Is life so dear, or peace so sweet, as to be purchased at the price of chains and slavery? Forbid it, Almighty God! I know not what course others may take, but as for me, give me liberty or give me death!

The implied message is, "You share my pride, therefore you will wish to share in my policy."

6. Shame

Shame is a feeling that you have been disgraced, or that other people think ill of you. It is often accompanied by regret; a wish that you had acted more wisely. It often leads to repentance; a resolution to do better in future.

Friends, dare we say we live in a law-abiding community when a young girl can be knocked down, beaten nearly to death, and robbed, in broad daylight on one of our main streets? Are there *men* in this city, where scores of people heard the victim's screams, and not one of them ran to help her? Are there *women* in this city, when not one would lift the telephone and call the police? And what are we to say about the witnesses of the crime, who declined to identify the assailant?

Friends, dare we say we are civilized, when an elderly man can fall down with a heart attack in the street, can lie there and die, while motorists drive serenely by, and while pedestrians, never heeding his moans, step over and around him?

Friends, let us drop the pretense that we are civilized. Let us admit that we are beasts, living in a jungle.

But let us resolve that we will not *remain* beasts. Let us resolve that our city shall not *remain* a jungle. Let us resolve to . . . etc.

An appeal to shame leads on to an appeal for action. The speaker makes the audience feel ashamed of themselves, and then suggests how they can relieve that feeling of shame.

7. Hope

Hope is the expectation of receiving benefits, or of being delivered from some unpleasantness. Hope deals, not with past or present, but with the future. It is the anticipation *now* of pleasurable emotions that one expects to enjoy later.

Hope of *gain* is one of the most common applications of this appeal. "This new Industrial Development Plan will bring new industry, new payrolls, new jobs, a new prosperity to this area. There will be new roads, new schools, new homes, new opportunity for everyone. So I urge you to vote. . . . etc."

The following example is taken from the speech of Edmund Burke to the British House of Lords, at the trial of Warren Hastings. Notice how, in the first paragraph of the excerpt, he arouses *fear*, then proceeds to arouse *hope*. (Remember that this speech was delivered at the time of the French Revolution, when the establishments of other countries felt that their hold on power was becoming precarious.)

My lords, the Commons will share in every fate with your lordships; there is nothing sinister which can happen to you, in which we shall not all be involved; and, if it should so happen that we shall be subjected to some of those frightful changes which we have seen—if it should happen that your lordships, stripped of all the decorous distinctions of human society, should, by hands at once base and cruel, be led to those scaffolds and machines of murder upon which great kings and glorious queens have shed their blood, amidst the prelates, amidst the nobles, amidst the magistrates, who supported their thrones—may you in those moments feel that consolation which I am persuaded they felt in the critical moments of their dreadful agony!

My lords, if you must fall, may you so fall! But, if you stand—and stand I trust you will—together with the fortune of this ancient monarchy, together with the ancient laws and liberties of this great and illustrious kingdom, may you stand as unimpeached in honor as in power; may you stand, not as a substitute for virtue, but as an ornament of virtue, as a security for virtue; may you stand long, and long stand the terror of tyrants; may you stand the refuge of afflicted nations; may you stand a sacred temple, for the perpetual residence of an inviolable justice.

(Note that the style of this speech would be unacceptable nowadays. We shall discuss style in Chapter 13.)

This example illustrates two important points in the use of emotional appeals—*contrast* and *duration*.

Contrast

An emotional appeal will seem stronger *if it is set in contrast with its opposite.* Here the *hopeful* image of the lasting power and influence of the Lords seems much brighter because it immediately follows the *fearful* image of the degradation and execution of the Lords.

Similarly an appeal to *pride* would be more powerful if it immediately followed an appeal to *shame.* Shakespeare was well aware of this. Immediately before the appeal to pride previously quoted from *Henry V*, he makes Henry say:

O, do not wish one more!
Rather proclaim it, Westmoreland, through my host,
That he which hath no stomach to this fight,
Let him depart; his passport shall be made

And crowns for convoy put into his purse:
We would not die in that man's company
That fears his fellowship to die with us.

Words such as "no stomach," "fears," "we would not die in
that man's company" produce here a strong suggestion of shame
which sets off, and heightens, the subsequent appeal to pride.

Use this principle of contrast whenever you can—contrast
hatred with love, grief with mirth, and so on.

Duration

The human mind does not willingly endure a strong emotion for
too long. When the limit is passed, the mind seeks refuge either in
apathy or in a contrasting emotion.

You have probably seen, in a poorly written movie or play, a
scene of horror and fear sustained too long. What happens? The
audience begins to laugh!

If, in making a speech, you praise someone too elaborately—
labor too long to make the audience admire him—you run the risk
of boring your listeners, and so arousing hostility toward your
hero, instead of admiration.

Burke does not go on too long with his arousal of fear before
changing to the mood of hope.

Bear this point in mind when framing your speeches. Emotional appeals should be the high spots of the speech, but you cannot risk keeping your audience in an emotional state too long. The
emotional appeals should be spaced out by calmer passages, using
the other demonstrative techniques described in Chapter 5.

8. Fear

Most people fear poverty, pain, disease and death. Such fears
serve as motive for suspicion, caution, prudence and thrift. You
will find that an appeal to fear is usually effective.

One glance around this audience shows that many of you are
overweight. Do you realize the dangers that you face? The excess
fat that you carry around all day increases your risk of suffering from
many diseases: heart and arterial degeneration, diabetes, high blood

pressure, cancer, arthritis, kidney disease, hernia, varicose veins and flat feet. Excess fat increases your risks in appendicitis, child birth, and all surgical operations. It predisposes to backaches. It makes you more susceptible to accidents of all kinds. Excess fat brings you needless suffering and premature death.

But there is a remedy. . . .

Here an appeal to fear, strong, yet not too long, is followed by an appeal to hope.

9. Desire

Desire for wealth and material possessions is one of the strongest motives in our society. Desire is akin to envy—a bitter feeling because someone else has something that you have not. Yet the appeal to desire is not necessarily degrading: it can be used for good purposes.

Ladies and Gentlemen, you have come to this meeting because you are dissatisfied with your position in life. You want to get more responsible jobs, increase your incomes, live in larger homes, and wear better clothes. You can achieve those aims, you can advance yourselves vocationally and financially, through the courses that will be offered at the proposed Adult Education Center. But if that Center is to be built, if you are to reap the benefits you desire, then the necessary referendum must pass by a sixty percent majority. So, at the next election . . .

10. Contentment

Contentment is the opposite of desire. It is a feeling of satisfaction with what you are or have, and an absence—at least a temporary absence—of desire.

Desire inspires *action,* to obtain the thing wanted; contentment leads to *inaction.* Naturally, if you are satisfied with things as they are, why should you rock the boat? So you sit still.

An appeal to contentment, then, will normally be appropriate if you want to avoid change.

Friends, fellow members, our club has never been so prosperous and so flourishing as during the past year. The mortgage on the club building has been paid off. While other similar clubs have raised their dues, our dues have remained unchanged. Attendance at our social events is up by fifteen percent over the ten year average. Our new publicity policy is attracting a very high caliber of new, young members, many of whom I'm pleased to see here at our annual meeting.

We've engaged a new chef for the dining room, and I know, from many conversations with members, that the quality of the food has improved as a result.

When I think of some of the stormy annual meetings we've had in the past, and contrast them with the smiles and good humor that prevail tonight, I think we have every reason to be satisfied with the way the club is being run.

So it gives me great pleasure to propose the re-election of. . . .

There is, in this speech, the implication: "You share my feeling of contentment, so you will feel inclined to support my motion."

Manner of Delivery

In using these techniques, your manner of delivery should be adapted to suit the emotion to which you are appealing. Obviously, it would be absurd to use the same pace, tone, facial expression, gesture, and posture in an appeal to grief as in an appeal to mirth.

There is no need to take acting lessons in "How to express hope," "How to look frightened," and so on. All you need do is *make yourself feel the emotion.* Then you will look and stand and speak in the way that best expresses that emotion.

Make yourself feel, and you will have no difficulty in making your audience feel with you.

The Desired Effect

An experienced speaker told me this anecdote. "After I had delivered a long persuasive speech, a woman came up to me and said, 'Your speech was all very interesting, but it was very obvious. I agree with all of it.'

"I was pleased to hear her comment, because that's just the effect I was aiming at—to make it all seem obvious."

The speaker was right. If your listeners think, "He's trying to persuade us," then you are not doing your work as well as you might.

But if they think, "Why, that's perfectly obvious. Anyone with half an eye could see that! Why didn't I think of it before?" then you are persuading effectively. Persuasion by emotional appeal is most likely to achieve this result.

Analysis of a Successful Speech

Let us analyze Mark Antony's speech, from *Julius Caesar (Act III, Scene 2)*. The language is Shakespeare's, but the substance of the speech was drawn from historical sources and it represents fairly accurately what Antony said. It is one of the most brilliant persuasive speeches on record.

The scene is Rome, the year, 44 B.C. There has just been a revolution. A band of aristocratic conspirators has hacked Julius Caesar to death, and has won the support of the citizens. Somewhat contemptuously, they permit Mark Antony to deliver a funeral oration for Caesar.

Antony comes on, accompanying Caesar's body, which is in a lidless coffin, covered with a cloak. The audience is hostile to him.

FOURTH CITIZEN: 'Twere well he speak no harm of Brutus here.

FIRST CITIZEN: This Caesar was a tyrant.

THIRD CITIZEN: Nay, that's certain. We are blest that Rome is rid of him.

It would be fatal (literally so) for Antony to say, "No, no! You're wrong. Caesar was not a tyrant. He was a good man, unjustly killed. You must believe me!" That would be meeting opposition head-on. See what he does say.

ANTONY: Friends, Romans, countrymen, lend me your ears;
          I come to bury Caesar, not to praise him.

He does not oppose the prejudice of the audience, but temporarily yields to it.

> The evil that men do lives after them;
> The good is oft interred with their bones.

A point of agreement—a general statement that no one is likely to oppose.

> So let it be with Caesar.

That is, "Let the good *he* did be buried with his bones: I am not going to say anything about it." Again Antony yields to the audience's prejudice, but gets in the thin end of the wedge, the suggestion that Caesar did do *some* good.

> The noble Brutus
> Hath told you Caesar was ambitious:

Another point of agreement.

> If it were so, it was a grievous fault.

Again yielding to prejudice, but, with the "if," planting a seed of doubt as to the grounds for the prejudice.

> And grievously hath Caesar answered it.
> Here, under leave of Brutus and the rest—
> For Brutus is an honorable man;
> So are they all, all honorable men—
> Come I to speak in Caesar's funeral.

Here ends the opening of the speech. It is a compound opening, built on a quotation and a timely reference. "The evil that men do," etc. is a quotation from Euripides, although Antony *reverses* the sense of what Euripides said, which was that the evil men do is buried with them, and the good lives on. It is not uncommon for a clever orator to twist a quotation to suit his purpose. The timely reference is "Brutus hath told you he was ambitious, etc."

Antony then announces his subject: "Come I to speak in Caesar's funeral" and launches into the Body of his speech.

> He was my friend, faithful and just to me

Here Antony begins a carefully-planned emotional appeal, which will eventually transform the citizens' hatred of the dead Caesar into love. The words "friend," "faithful and just" are used for their emotional connotations.

> But Brutus says he was ambitious;
> And Brutus is an honorable man.
> He hath brought many captives home to Rome,
> Whose ransoms did the general coffers fill.

This is an appeal to the citizens' *pride,* and to *desire*—these victories glorified your country; these ransoms were profitable to you. Note how this brings an element of *personal concern* into the speech.

> Did this in Caesar seem ambitious?

He is still being tactful. He does not say, "This proves that Caesar was not ambitious." He puts it to the audience as a question.

> When that the poor have cried, Caesar hath wept.

Another emotional appeal.

> Ambition should be made of sterner stuff:
> Yet Brutus says he was ambitious,
> And Brutus is an honorable man.

He is conceding again, rather than challenging. Antony has not yet won over the audience. Note the repetition of the "honorable Brutus" idea.

> You all did see that on the Lupercal
> I thrice presented him a kingly crown
> Which he did thrice refuse. Was this ambition?

Not, "I'm telling you that..." but *"You all did see..."* This is citing an example to demonstrate his first point, which is "Caesar was not ambitious."

> Yet Brutus says he was ambitious,

Conflict between the facts and Brutus's allegation.

> And sure, he is an honorable man.

Note how the excessive praise of Brutus becomes, in effect, a criticism.

> I speak not to disprove what Brutus spoke,
> But here I am to speak what I do know.

Now he moves on to his second point: "Caesar loved the Roman people."

> You all did love him once, not without cause:

He develops his emotional appeal a little further: "You *did* love him once."

> What cause withholds you then to mourn for him?
> Oh, judgment! thou are fled to brutish beats,
> And men have lost their reason. Bear with me:
> My heart is in the coffin there with Caesar,
> And I must pause till it come back to me.

He pauses and weeps—another appeal to emotion. The citizens begin to be swayed. "Methinks there is much reason in his sayings," etc. Note this reaction. The people have been swayed by emotion, but *they say* they are yielding to reason! People like to believe they are reasonable, even when they are not.

Antony recovers and continues with his second point.

> But here's a parchment with the seal of Caesar;
> I found it in his closet, 'tis his will:

An exhibit!

> Let but the commons hear this testament—
> Which, pardon me, I do not mean to read—
> And they would go and kiss dead Caesar's wounds
> And dip their napkins in his sacred blood. . . .

A strong appeal to the curiosity of the audience. They demand to hear the will. If he had tried to read it to them at the start, he might have aroused opposition. Someone might have said, "It's a forgery!" But his technique forestalls all such opposition. He makes them *want* to hear it.

> Have patience, gentle friends, I must not read it;
> It is not meet you know how Caesar loved you. . . .

There is conflict between their desire to hear, and his feigned reluctance to read the will. Conflict heightens interest.

> 'Tis good you know not that you are his heirs;
> For if you should, Oh, what would come of it!

More emotional appeals: he arouses their *desire,* hinting that they have a legacy coming to them. The citizens loudly demand to hear the will.

> Will you be patient? Will you stay awhile?
> I have o'ershot myself to tell you of it.
> I fear I wrong the honorable men
> Whose daggers have stabbed Caesar. . . . .

The emotional appeal is heightened by the suspense. It is now clear that he is being ironic—saying one thing and meaning the opposite—when he talks of "honorable men." The crowd will now accept this irony. They again demand to hear the will.

> You will compel me, then, to read the will?
> Then make a ring around the corpse of Caesar,
> And let me show you him that made the will. . . . .
> If you have tears, prepare to shed them now.

He begins to stir up feelings of grief in his listeners.

> You all do know this mantle: I remember
> The first time ever Caesar put it on;
> 'Twas on a summer's evening, in his tent
> That day he overcame the Nervii.

Another exhibit—the cloak—serves to distract the audience from the will. The victory over the Nervii is mentioned as an appeal to national pride.

Antony points out, rent by rent, where the conspirators' daggers ripped the mantle, then opens his third point: "You, citizens of Rome, should feel love for the dead Caesar."

> Kind souls, what, weep you when you but behold
> Our Caesar's vesture wounded? Look you here,
> Here is himself, marr'd as you see, with traitors.

He flings off the cloak, exposing the mangled corpse. Another exhibit! Note the timing. The key exhibit is revealed *after* the emotions of the audience were thoroughly aroused. This, too, is the moment to slip in the word "traitors"—the first time he has ventured to use such a strong expression for the conspirators.

The crowd becomes highly excited and is now ready to riot against the conspirators. Antony checks them.

> Good friends, sweet friends, let me not stir you up
> To such a sudden flood of mutiny.

Antony's next point: "You should mutiny against the conspirators" is stated—as a clever orator will often state a controversial point—in the *negative*. He says, "Don't mutiny" but he means "Do mutiny."

> They that have done the deed are honorable:
> What private griefs they have, alas, I know not,
> That made them do it: they are wise and honorable,
> And will, no doubt, with reasons answer you.

Further repetition of the "honorable" deepens the irony. This is to damn with excess praise.

> I come not, friends, to steal away your hearts:
> I am no orator, as Brutus is;
> But, as you know me all, a plain blunt man,
> That love my friend; and that they know full well
> That gave me public leave to speak of him;
> For I have neither wit, nor words, nor worth,
> Action nor utterance, nor the power of speech,
> To stir men's blood: I only speak right on;

The passage from "Good friends, sweet friends" to "only speak right on" seems rather dull and quiet. It is deliberately made so. Remember what we said earlier, that an audience cannot remain too long in the grip of an emotion. So he deliberately calms them, before proceeding to his conclusion which will raise them to a still higher pitch of emotion.

> I tell you that which you yourselves do know;
> Show you sweet Caesar's wounds, poor poor dumb mouths,

And bid them speak for me: but were I Brutus,
And Brutus Antony, there were an Antony
Would ruffle up your spirits and put a tongue
In every wound of Caesar that should move
The stones of Rome to rise and mutiny.

Again the point, "You should mutiny" is stated indirectly. The citizens are now wildly excited; they are about to burn Brutus's house and lynch the conspirators. Again Antony checks them. Again he will calm them, and again, with a strong appeal to desire, will arouse them to the greatest possible emotional intensity.

Why, friends, you go to do you know not what;
Wherein hath Caesar thus deserved your loves?
Alas, you know not: I must tell you, then:
You have forgot the will I told you of. . . .
Here is the will, and under Caesar's seal.
To every Roman citizen he gives,
To every several man, seventy-five drachmas.

An appeal to desire. The citizens cry vengeance.

Moreover, he hath left you all his walks,
His private arbors and new-planted orchards
On this side Tiber; he hath left them you
And to your heirs for ever, common pleasures,
To walk abroad and recreate yourselves.
Here was a Caesar! When comes such another?

Pointing again at the corpse, he ends on a strong rhetorical question. It is a safe question, by the way, framed so that there cannot be an unfavorable answer from the crowd. Antony makes no further attempt to restrain the citizens; they rush off to attack Brutus and the conspirators.

Let us review the structure of this speech.

Opening: Quotation and timely reference.
Body: Point 1. Caesar was not ambitious, so Brutus's
                    excuse for killing him is invalid.
              Point 2. Caesar loved the Roman people.
              Point 3. You, citizens of Rome, should feel love
                    for the dead Caesar.

Point 4. You should avenge Caesar by mutinying
against the conspirators.
Conclusion: Review: Caesar loved you.
Caesar's wounds cry "Mutiny!"
Gratitude urges you, "Mutiny!"

I have quoted here only a part of Antony's speech. If you read
it for yourself and analyze it line by line, you will find it a perfect
model of the appeal to emotion, and a perfect example of how to
deal with a hostile audience.

Summary

An emotional appeal is the quickest, surest way to demonstrate
a point.

Emotional appeals are appropriate and ethical in public speaking.

Ten useful emotional appeals:

1. Love
2. Hatred
3. Mirth
4. Grief
5. Pride
6. Shame
7. Hope
8. Fear
9. Desire
10. Contentment

Through emotional appeals you gain power to persuade.

Set one emotional appeal in contrast to its opposite.

Don't sustain an emotional appeal too long.

Feel an emotion yourself and you will easily convey it to others.

Exercises

1. Review the speeches that you have prepared or delivered
earlier. See where they could be strengthened by inclusion of emo-

tional appeals. Incorporate such appeals where appropriate, and deliver the speeches again in practice sessions.

2. Imagine you are a trade-union official addressing your members, trying to persuade them to seek longer paid vacations instead of a raise, in forthcoming contract negotiations. What emotional appeals could you use? Write appropriate notes for this part of the speech.

3. Imagine you are the mayor of a city, addressing a meeting of voters, urging the passing of a referendum for construction of a new library-museum building. What emotional appeals could you use? Write appropriate notes for this part of the speech.

7. The Conclusion of the Speech

Great is the art of beginning, but greater the art is of ending.

HENRY WADSWORTH LONGFELLOW

It could be said that the opening and body of the speech are only preparation for the conclusion. The conclusion is your last contact with the audience (unless there is a question-answer period); it is your last chance to impress your personality and ideas on the audience. A weak conclusion will more or less destroy the effect of a good opening and body. A strong conclusion will confirm and multiply that effect. It is worth taking the trouble to plan your conclusion carefully and deliver it effectively.

How Not to Conclude

1. You will sometimes hear a speaker work through the body of his speech, demonstrate and recapitulate his last point, then simply say, "Thank you" and sit down. That is not *concluding*; it is simply *stopping*.

"Thank you" seems to be used by some speakers as a way of letting the audience know they have finished. It is weak. A proper conclusion leaves no doubt that the speaker has finished.

2. Don't end with an apology.

Mr. Chairman, I'm afraid I've gone on too long, and I will sit down before I strain the patience of the audience too far.

Ladies and Gentlemen, I haven't fully covered the subject. It would be impossible to cover it properly in the time at my disposal.

But perhaps the few rambling thoughts that I have uttered will rouse a question or two in the mind of some listener.

Such apologies leave the audience feeling thoroughly depressed.

3. Don't bring on yourself the "guillotine" conclusion by going on so long that the chairman has to intervene and shut you up before you have finished.

How to Conclude

Remember how we described the functions of opening, body and conclusion:

The opening: Tell them what you're going to tell them.

The body: Tell them.

Conclusion: Tell them what you've told them.

So in concluding, you will be seeking means to remind the audience of what you have told them.

Plan your conclusion. Don't leave it to the inspiration of the moment. Here are six tested techniques; one of them will serve your purpose.

Summary

Recapitulate the main points of your speech. This method is appropriate where your aim is to impart information or to inspire belief. Here is the conclusion from a speech I made on "Writing Non-Fiction Books" to an audience of writers and would-be writers.

Non-fiction book publishers are flourishing now, and there is plenty of opportunity, and plenty of money to be made, in the writing of non-fiction books.

But librarians are invading the publishing business with their photographic and electronic copying devices. Most librarians are completely unscrupulous in their violations of copyright law.

If copies of your books are multiplied without payment, you cannot afford to write; you cannot live. So unless the librarians' abuse of copyright is checked, non-fiction writing is doomed.

In the body of the speech, of course, I had demonstrated the various points by means of examples—statistics, quotations, etc. In the conclusion I summed them up rapidly to refresh the listeners' memory of them.

Anecdote

Tell an anecdote that vividly illustrates the theme of your speech. This method is not often used, because suitable anecdotes are not easily found.

The anecdote must be *pointed,* so that the audience grasps its meaning in a flash. If you have to follow it up with explanations and comments, you will find your conclusion tailing off weakly.

The anecdote must be *strong*—stronger than any anecdote you have used earlier in the speech: that is, it must be richer in significance, and must more clearly and powerfully express the emotional tone of your speech than any other anecdote you have told.

Here, for example, is the concluding anecdote from a speech on "Literary Success." The theme of the speech is "Hard, persistent work is the secret of literary success."

When Honoré de Balzac was arrested for debt, he did not sulk or despair. He set up a table in the common room of the debtors' prison and there, amid the stench and uproar of several hundred men, women and children eating, drinking, laughing, crying, gambling, loving and dying, he calmly and quietly got on with his work.

Quotation

The quotation serves much the same purpose as the anecdote, and it must similarly be pointed and strong. Suppose you were making a speech on "Juvenile Delinquency" with the theme, "Milder legislation and more understanding are needed in the treatment of juvenile delinquents." Your conclusion could incorporate an apt quotation from Charles Dickens.

Ladies and Gentlemen, the measures that I'm suggesting are not new-fangled notions dreamed up by do-gooders; they are simply the expression of common sense, common kindness and common humanity. They are the measures called for by Charles Dickens over a century ago. "Give us, in mercy, better homes when we're a-lying in our cradles; give us better food when we're a-working for our lives; give us kinder laws to bring us back when we're a-going wrong; and don't set Jail, Jail, Jail afore us everywhere we turn."

Question

Instead of giving your listeners a concluding thought, make them conjure up the thought themselves, by ending with an appropriate question or series of questions. This conclusion is particularly appropriate when you wish to arouse emotion concerning the theme, but you have no clear line of action to recommend.

And so we see that, in our community, religion is a declining influence on education, literature, family life and politics. How much longer can this decline continue? In ten years, in twenty years, how much influence will our religion still possess? And what is our church doing to check the decline? What are *you* doing about it?

Call for Action

This method, of course, should be used when the purpose of your speech is to obtain action. If you are seeking votes for a candidate, donations for a charity, signatures on a petition, then end with a direct call for votes, donations or signatures.

Here, from Act III, Scene 1 of Shakespeare's *King Henry V,* is the conclusion of a speech in which Henry is urging his troops to advance boldly into the breech at Harfleur.

> I see you stand like greyhounds in the slips,
> Straining upon the start. The game's afoot;
> Follow your spirit, and upon this charge
> Cry, "God for Harry, England and Saint George."

Statement of the Theme

It will sometimes happen, as we have seen already, that you will go through the opening and body of your speech without ever specifically stating the theme. If you have done this, then a strong, clear statement of the theme makes a good conclusion.

Here, for example is the conclusion of the Gettysburg Address:

... we here highly resolve that these dead shall not have died in vain; that this nation, under God, shall have a new birth of freedom; and that government of the people, by the people, for the people, shall not perish from the earth.

Maintain Power

Some speakers have a tendency, when they have finshed with the body of the speech, to diminish, little by little, the vocal power they are using. This results in a dwindling, dying conclusion. The deaf lady in the back row does not hear it. The people who do hear it get the impression that the speaker is running out of steam; they are not properly impressed by the words of his conclusion.

Avoid this weak habit. Be sure that you maintain full vocal power right up to the last word. If it is by any means appropriate, increase your power, so that you conclude somewhat above the average power level you have used throughout.

A strong conclusion heightens the effect of your speech.

After the Speech

Correct behavior after the last word is spoken can add considerably to the impression that your speech makes on the audience.

1. *Don't* sit down, or scurry away from the lectern, immediately after you have finished speaking. Haste to get away from your speaking position creates a strong impression of nervousness.

2. *Don't* turn to the chairman with some apologetic remark: ''I hope, Mr. Chairman, that I didn't run too far over my time.''

3. *Do* remain at the lectern, or table, or microphone, exactly in the spot where you delivered your speech.

4. Repeat the eye contact which you made before you began. Sweep your eyes over the audience, to left, to right, and back to the center. Hold your gaze there.

5. *Say nothing.*

6. Do nothing—Don't start rustling and shuffling your notes to get them ready for removal. Don't straighten your necktie or your hair.

7. Give a slight smile (unless the occasion is unusually solemn).

8. Wait for the applause. If your conclusion has been very strong, you may have to wait several seconds. But keep waiting, and the applause will come.

This technique is important. It increases the amount of applause that you will receive. Moreover, it increases your reputation as a speaker, because it leaves with the audience a final impression that you are experienced and perfectly confident.

Summary

Plan and deliver a strong, meaningful conclusion.
Six techniques for a conclusion are:
    1. Summary
    2. Anecdote
    3. Quotation
    4. Question
    5. Call for action
    6. Statement of the theme
Maintain vocal power right to the last word.
After concluding, stand still and wait for the applause.

Exercises

1. Review the speeches you have prepared or delivered earlier. See how you could strengthen them by using more effective conclusions.

2. Make notes of the conclusions delivered by other speakers in practice sessions. See if you can find ways to improve them.

3. Imagine you are appealing for funds in aid of a charity of your choice. What conclusion would you use? Write appropriate notes for this part of the speech.

4. Look through your daily newspaper for a controversial subject. Prepare and deliver a speech, taking one side or the other of that subject. Provide a strong conclusion designed to convert listeners to your point of view, or make them take the action you recommend.

8. Developing Self-Confidence

Be of good courage.

ISAIAH

Fear prevents many people from ever speaking in public; to many who do speak, fear continues to be a more or less severe handicap. That is a pity, because if they set about it in the right way, they could develop self-confidence, speak more effectively than they do now, and enjoy speaking instead of dreading it. This chapter offers some hints that will enable you to eliminate fear on the platform.

The Signs and Symptoms of Fear

Fear is an unpleasant state of mind. We shall understand it better if we remember that mind and body are not separate, but are parts of the same entity, like the ignition and fuel systems of an internal combustion motor.

Fear disturbs not only the mind, but also the whole mind-body entity. Fear impairs the functioning of mind and body. These mental and physical impairments are all parts of the same phenomenon. Let us examine them.

1. Morbid concentration on some subject associated with the fear. For example:

"Suppose I can't make myself heard."

"Suppose I forget what I'm going to say."

"Suppose I make myself look stupid to the audience."

"Suppose someone asks me a question I can't answer."

2. Loss of memory. The anxious thought, so tenaciously held, ousts from the conscious mind the ideas that you need for beginning and continuing the speech.

3. Trembling of hands and limbs.

4. Sweating of palms, body and face.

5. Cringing posture: knees bent, back bowed, head hanging.

6. Facial pallor.

7. Shifting gaze: inability to look at the audience; a strong desire to look at the floor or ceiling, or out of the windows.

8. Quick, shallow pulse.

9. Falling blood pressure.

10. Abnormal thirst; dryness of the mouth and throat.

11. Poor control of the voice: squeaky tone, stuttering, nervous giggling, or even temporary dumbness.

12. In extreme cases, fainting.

What Not to Do

1. I have heard it suggested that a speaker can gain confidence by despising his audience, by turning over in his mind such thoughts as:

"The poor boobs, how stupid they are! They know nothing about the subject, but I—the great expert—will enlighten them."

Or, "They all owe me money, and they have come humbly to beg for more time to repay."

Or, "They have all lost their clothes, and are sitting in their underwear. I am the only person properly dressed, so I feel confident."

These methods are unsound because:

a) You know the statements are not true. Genuine confidence will not be built on a lie.

b) Possibly, by concentrating hard enough on a known falsehood, you can temporarily believe it. But your mind would be better occupied by dwelling on something more constructive. (We shall discuss some possibilities later.)

c) A good speaker-audience relationship should be built on mutual respect. You cannot give your best effort and thought to people whom—even half-heartedly—you despise.

So I do not recommend any form of mocking, critical thought towards the audience. Give them *respect*: give them the feeling that you like them.

2. Don't drink alcohol or take tranquilizers before you speak. A drug may suppress your fear, but it will probably make you *too* calm and relaxed, robbing you of that moderate excitement and tension which stimulate you and help you to give your best on the platform. Moreover, the drug will certainly blunt and slow down your thinking.

3. Don't say anything that tells the audience you are nervous or inexperienced. For example, don't pause after a few sentences and ask, "Can you hear me?" It is your business to speak so that you *know* you are being heard.

How to Speak Confidently

Remember that mind and body are parts of the same entity, like the two wings of an airplane. If one ascends, the other ascends with it. So here is a system by which you can make mind and body work together to produce unshakable self-confidence.

In Advance

1. Research and think carefully: make yourself *an authority* on the subject. The knowledge that you are better informed than the audience, that you have something useful and interesting to offer them, builds confidence.

2. Write or type clear, orderly notes. The opening and closing sentences may be written out verbatim if you wish. Certainly quotations should be written out. The remainder of the speech should be covered by brief notes of key ideas. Well-prepared notes build confidence; you know that you cannot lose the thread of your speech.

3. If you are using visual aids, thoroughly rehearse your handling of them.

Before You Mount the Platform

4. If you can, walk about a bit. Gentle exercise deepens your breathing, draws blood away from the brain to the muscles of the legs, and so counters any tendency toward fear.

5. Take several deep, sighing breaths, then yawn. Repeat the routine several times. Here we are utilizing the mind-body concept. Yawning is a physical sign of relaxation, calmness and comfort. So by inducing a yawn in the body, you make your mind feel calm and at ease. At this time, dwell on a thought such as this: "I am breathing deeply, charging my blood with oxygen. This will give me strength and vocal power on the platform. The audience wants to hear me. I will make sure that they do hear me!"

6. Review your notes. Usually the chairman, or whoever is in charge of the meeting, knows that a speaker wants a few minutes to collect his thoughts at this time. But if the chairman does not offer you the chance to think, if he occupies you in chit-chat, or lets other people do so, then tell him, "Mr. Chairman, do you mind if I break off the conversation now, and take a few minutes to look over my notes?"

On the Platform Before You Speak

7. Guard against the tendency to slip back into shallow breathing. Partial oxygen starvation induces anxiety and fear. Continue to breathe slowly and deeply. Thorough oxygenation of the blood has a powerful calming effect on the mind. (But don't permit yourself to yawn on the platform!)

Inexperienced speakers may sometimes have an outburst of nervous giggling when they stand up to speak. This is not genuine mirth. It is an attempt—by the gasping which follows each giggle —to get more oxygen. The preparatory deep breathing will obviate the need for giggling.

8. While waiting your turn to speak, devote your full attention to what is being said by the chairman, or by speakers who precede you on the program. You are thoroughly prepared and need not, for the moment, think further about what you are going to say.

9. When it is nearly time for you to speak, begin to repeat mentally, and dwell on the meaning of, your opening sentence. Keep this up without pause, until you rise to your feet. The conscious mind can hold only one idea at a time. So, if you keep it occupied with the first thing you intend to say, it will have no room for thoughts of fear.

10. When the chairman calls you to speak, assume an erect posture, with spine straight, shoulders back and head up. Again you utilize the mind-body concept. A feeling of confidence naturally

produces an erect, alert posture. So, conversely, if you force your body to *look* calm and fearless, you induce a feeling of calmness and confidence in the mind. If you have to move to the lectern or microphone, don't rush and fall over something—move slowly and calmly.

During Your Speech

11. Deliver the salutation loudly, clearly and slowly. This is the moment when the listener gets his first impression of you, and forms either the idea, "Oh, dear! I'm afraid I won't be able to hear him very well," or "Good! I'm sure I'll be able to hear everything this speaker says."

Watch the effect of a loud, clear salutation on an audience: a visible relaxation, accompanied by little smiles of relief. Their feeling of pleasure reacts upon you and gives you confidence.

12. Except on the most solemn occasions, smile at the audience as you deliver the salutation. As you exhibit one of the signs of calmness and confidence—a smile—you *feel* calm and confident.

13. Don't be ashamed of your notes. When you want to look at them raise them boldly. If you temporarily lose the thread of your speech, take your time; look at the notes until you find the next thing you want to say. The listener does not mind seeing you look at your notes. He knows that is the reason you have them. He is content to revolve in his mind, for a few seconds, the thought you gave him before you paused.

Hold the notes tightly; don't drop them. The feel of them between your fingers, with the knowledge that they contain all you need for your speech, builds confidence.

Similarly, if you are using a lectern, don't try to smuggle your notes on to it without letting the audience see them; don't try to conceal your action when you turn to a new sheet.

14. The first few times you speak, you may find that the gaze of the audience embarrasses you. An easy cure is to avoid looking into their eyes. Instead, direct your gaze a few inches above the heads of the people in the back row. (*Not* up at the ceiling!) Keep your eyes moving from side to side at that altitude. Few of the audience will perceive that you are not looking at them. But this should be only a temporary crutch. As soon as you can, practice looking right into the eyes of the audience.

Prepare yourself for this by thinking in advance, "I want

the audience to look at me. I'll be glad when they look at me. That means that I have their full attention.''

(The time to worry, indeed, is when people *stop* looking at you. That is a danger signal; it usually means either that they are bored, or that they cannot hear you.)

15. Don't hesitate to keep pausing for breath whenever you need it. Well-filled lungs produce a strong, pleasant toned voice. Thorough oxygenation of the blood produces calmness and confidence.

16. Don't hesitate to pause for thought, or to find the right word. The audience does not mind. If, during a lengthy speech, your throat gets dry, pause while you pour and drink some water. Take your time! Do it confidently and openly. As long as all of them can see what you are doing, the audience's attention will be riveted on you. Don't try to drink and speak at the same time; this will probably induce an embarrassing spell of coughing or choking.

17. Continue to speak loudly, slowly and clearly. Low volume, haste and indistinctness are signs of nervousness. But if your voice *sounds* confident, you will tend to *feel* confident.

General Hints on Developing Confidence

Take every opportunity to speak before an audience. It helps you to get used to the sound of your own voice, and to having other people watch you as you speak. Ask a question, for example, or simply stand up and say, briefly, how much you have enjoyed the speech. Take part in debates. The more speaking you do, the more confident you will feel.

But never eliminate, or try to eliminate, all feeling of excitement before you speak. This is different from fear. Fear tends to paralyze, or at least to hamper, the action of mind and body. A moderate, pleasant excitement stimulates your heart, your breathing and your mind, and makes you speak better.

Summary

Fear can be replaced by self-confidence.
Respect your audience.
Don't take drugs or alcohol to suppress fear.

To speak confidently:
1. Become an authority on your subject.
2. Prepare clear, orderly, comprehensive notes.
3. Rehearse handling of visual aids.
4. Exercise gently before the meeting.
5. Breathe deeply before the meeting.
6. Review your notes before the meeting.
7. On the platform, keep breathing deeply, slowly.
8. Pay attention to other speakers.
9. Just before you speak, review your opening sentence.
10. When you are called, stand erect.
11. Deliver the salutation loudly, clearly, slowly.
12. Smile at the audience.
13. Use your notes boldly.
14. Keep your eyes on the audience.
15. Keep breathing deeply as you speak.
16. Don't be afraid to pause.
17. Keep speaking loudly, slowly, clearly.

Practice in speaking builds self-confidence.

Moderate excitement makes you speak better.

Exercise

From now on, you can execute items 1-6 in the list every time you speak. Of the remaining items, select two or three that you know you need the most. Copy them in big letters on each sheet of your notes, so that you will be constantly reminded of them. Continue with this until you apply those hints easily and automatically. Then proceed to apply two or three more items in the same way, until you have mastered them all.

9. Breathing

Some of us are out of breath.

LEWIS CARROLL

Breath is the basis of health. Deep breathing purifies and oxygenates the blood, gives vigor to the body, and tends to promote long life. Deep breathing steadies the nerves. This chapter, as well as helping you speak better, can save you thousands of dollars in druggist's and doctor's bills.

Breath and Voice

Breath is basic to your voice. If your breathing habits are good, so is your voice. If, like most people, you breathe shallowly and irregularly, your voice will be thin and weak; you will not be able to project it so as to fill a big room. You will not have full control over your voice. You will soon tire; you will be unable to deliver long speeches at full power.

But if you make a little effort and establish correct breathing habits, you will become a powerful speaker. You will develop, not only a powerful, long lasting voice, but also, you will develop the physical stamina to make long speeches, and to keep thinking hard as you speak. Let there be no mistake about it, public speaking is hard work, hard physically as well as mentally! But, with correct breathing, you can do that work *and enjoy it.*

105

How Not to Breathe

Two common methods of breathing are unsuitable for public speakers.

1. *Shoulder-breathing.* The speaker raises his shoulders to inhale, lowers them to exhale. This produces only a slight variation in lung capacity.

2. *Chest-breathing.* The speaker raises and lowers the upper part of his chest. This is sometimes called "military breathing," because to do it you have to keep sticking your chest out like a soldier on parade. It is better than shoulder-breathing, but is still far from the best method.

Both shoulder- and chest-breathing tend to produce excessive tension in the shoulder and chest muscles. This tension soon tires a speaker and gives his voice a thin, harsh tone.

Some speakers combine both shoulder- and chest-breathing. This is better than either method used separately, but still produces tension and poor tone, and still gives far less than the maximum intake of air.

The Best Way

The best breathing system for speakers uses the diaphragm, which is a sheet of muscle lying across the body just about at the level of the arch formed by the lower ribs. At rest, the diaphragm is dished upward, like an inverted washbowl. When it contracts, its center moves downward.

For simplicity, think of the body as a cylinder; the upper part is the chest, the lower part the abdomen. The diaphragm is a piston moving up and down—not all the way, but through the middle third of the cylinder. With the diaphragm lowered, at the bottom of its stroke, the volume of the chest is at its maximum. As the diaphragm rises, the volume of the chest decreases. As the diaphragm sinks again, the volume of the chest increases once more.

These changes of volume are achieved without any muscular effort of the upper chest, shoulders or neck, solely by moving the diaphragm. And these changes of volume are *much greater* than any change you can make by trying to expand and contract the relatively rigid structure of the upper chest.

The lungs, which fill most of your chest, are spongy in texture. As the volume of the chest increases, they absorb air; as the volume of the chest decreases, they expel it.

So, solely by moving your diaphragm—which, by the way, is a very powerful muscle, flexible and easy to move—you achieve a copious inflow and outflow of air.

Learning to Use the Diaphragm

If you are not accustomed to diaphragm-breathing, try this exercise, and you will easily learn to do it. Wear clothing that is not tight around the waist.

1. Stand erect, with your left hand pressed against the front of your body, the root of your little finger over your navel.

2. Keep your shoulders and upper chest relaxed. Try not to move these parts at all during the exercise.

3. Breathe out steadily, until your lungs feel quite empty. As the diaphragm rises, you will feel your hand moving inward, toward your backbone.

4. Now breathe in, without moving shoulders or upper chest. As the diaphragm flattens and descends, you will feel your hand being pushed outward, away from your backbone.

5. Repeat the exercise twenty times, so that you get the feel of the moving diaphragm.

6. Then take your hand away and breathe twenty times, still with shoulder and chest muscles relaxed.

7. Repeat the whole exercise daily until you can breathe with your diaphragm any time you wish to do so.

Then proceed to the following exercises.

Breathing Exercises

You do not have to do these exercises in numerical order. Mix them up; give yourself variety; use whichever is most convenient. But keep using them for the rest of your life. You will prolong that life, and enjoy it more, because you are healthier. Moreover, you will be helping to develop a rich, powerful voice.

Exercise 1

1. When sitting or lying down, inhale fully to the count of 4. You can count seconds if you wish or, better, count your own heartbeats.
2. Hold the lungs full while you count 2.
3. Exhale completely to the count of 4.
4. Hold the lungs empty to the count of 2.
5. Inhale to the count of 4 and repeat the cycle.

If you are counting heartbeats you will notice, after a few cycles of this exercise, that your heart is slowing down. This is a desirable result. Inadequate oxygenation of the blood tends to produce a quick heartbeat; thorough oxygenation of the blood produces a slower heartbeat.

When you are comfortable with the 4-2-4-2 count, change to a count of 6-3-6-3. When you have mastered that—when you can do it without the slightest strain—change to 8-4-8-4.

Proceed just as far as you like with this exercise. So long as you develop steadily, stage by stage, you can do yourself only good. You may eventually reach 16-8-16-8.

Slow, deep breathing has a soothing effect on the nerves. If you are tense or fearful, sit down or lie down, do fifteen or twenty cycles of this exercise. You will feel noticeably calmer, more cheerful and more confident.

Try it at night, when you are in bed. It will help to put you to sleep. Try it at work; it will give you new energy, and will help to reduce any strain and tension that your job is causing.

Exercise 2

1. When walking, inhale fully to the count of 4, counting your footsteps.
2. Hold the lungs full to the count of 2.
3. Exhale completely to the count of 4.
4. Inhale to the count of 4 and repeat the cycle.

Note that, while walking or otherwise exercising, you do not hold the lungs empty but, as soon as the exhalation is complete, you begin to breathe in again. Similarly, once you are used to the 4-2-4, 4-2-4 cycle, you can increase it to 6-3-6, then to 8-4-8 and so on.

Exercise 3

Exercises 1 and 2 will increase the capacity and efficiency of your respiratory system. Now we come to some exercises that will help you use that capacity effectively in speaking.

1. Exhale completely.
2. Inhale fully.
3. Now sound a vowel—ah, ee or oo—and sustain it as long as you can until your lungs are empty.
4. Fill your lungs again and repeat the exercise.
   When you produce the vowel sound, listen for these qualities:
   a) Steadiness—that is, freedom from quavering in pitch.
   b) Clear, resonant tone—no rasping, no "breathy" sound.
   c) Constant power.

Exercise 4

This is the same as Exercise 3, except that you vary the power of the sound. Begin with the least possible power, increase to the highest power you can attain without shouting, then fade away to the least possible power just before your breath is exhausted.

Exercise 5

This is an exercise for duration.

1. Exhale completely.
2. Inhale fully.
3. Begin counting, as fast as you can, in a loud, clear, speaking voice, articulating all the numbers distinctly. Control your expenditure of breath and see how far you can count.
4. Repeat several times daily until you can count to 60 on one breath.

Exercise 6

1. Find a piece of prose or poetry that you enjoy. Stand up and hold the book ready for reading.
2. Exhale completely.

3. Inhale fully.

4. Begin reading in a loud, clear, speaking voice, with full expression.

5. Just before your first breath is exhausted, find a convenient spot in the text for a brief pause. Inhale as fast as you can, and continue reading.

6. Just before your second breath is exhausted, pause, inhale and continue.

7. See how far you get with three breaths.

8. Repeat daily, trying by improved breath control to read more and more of the passage with three breaths.

Breathing On the Platform

For speaking, don't wear clothes that are unduly tight about the waist; they stop your diaphragm from working freely, and keep you short of breath.

Begin deep breathing *before* you start to speak. This steadies your nerves and stimulates your thought processes.

Normally you snatch quick breaths during short pauses between phrases or sentences. But when you make a long pause—say after recapitulating one of the main points of your speech—seize the opportunity for a deep, slow breath as you look at your notes.

Never let yourself remain short of breath. If you do find yourself temporarily short of breath, pause—even if it means extending an end-of-sentence pause—and take in all the air you need. The audience will not notice the extra pause, so long as you maintain a calm expression; but they will notice the stronger voice and the more confident manner that follow from deep, steady breathing.

Summary

Correct breathing produces vocal power and physical stamina.
Shoulder-breathing and chest-breathing are inadequate.
Diaphragm-breathing is the easiest and best method.
Exercise to develop deep, automatic diaphragm-breathing.
Slow, deep breathing soothes the nerves.
Never let yourself get short of breath while speaking.

10. Developing and Using the Voice

You must articulate every syllable distinctly.
LORD CHESTERFIELD

Your voice gives the audience an impression of your character. A weak voice suggests weak thoughts and arguments; a mumbling, slurred voice suggests feeble intelligence. In a few seconds—long before the audience has had time to weigh the merits of what you say—your voice creates an emotional reaction, and makes some, at least, of the audience like you or dislike you.

This may not be logical or fair; but it is true. You have to approach the audience *on their terms,* and one of those terms is that they expect to hear a comprehensible, pleasant voice.

You can acquire such a voice. Your voice is not a fixed feature like your nose. Voice is a *function,* produced by the vibration of the vocal cords in your larynx, shaped and amplified in your mouth and head.

Your voice is made anew from moment to moment. A bad voice is not a permanent handicap: it is just *a bad habit*! If you are not satisfied with your voice, you can improve it.

Common Vocal Problems

1. *"Thinking-noises."* Some speakers make non-verbal noises when they pause to think. "Er" and "Ah" are the commonest of these thinking-noises. Other speakers make sucking or tutting sounds.

111

The peculiar thing about these sounds is that *the speaker never knows he is making them*. He concentrates so intensely that he does not hear himself. But the noises are noticeable to the audience. They create the impression that the speaker doesn't quite know what he is talking about. They weaken the effect of his speech.

In a class, the teacher will warn you when you make thinking-noises. If you have no teacher, ask a friend to listen for the noises.

If you are making them, stop at once. Every time, before you begin to speak, say to yourself, "Whenever I pause to think, I will keep my mouth shut." Form the habit of *silence* when you pause. Listen to yourself during pauses.

Write on every page of your notes, "N.T.N." It means "No Thinking-Noises." It will be a reminder to you but if other people see your notes, they will not know what it means.

Spare no pains to conquer this habit: your speeches will at once become more pleasing and more effective.

2. *Lip-smacking.* Some speakers, if their lips become dry, moisten them during pauses. This is acceptable, if it is done silently. But if the lips are parted quickly, they may produce a smacking sound. Here again, the speaker is unaware of what he is doing.

Listen to yourself, get a friend to listen, too, and conquer this habit. Form the new habit of moistening the lips silently; wedge the lips apart with a slight forward movement of your tongue.

3. *Swallowed Voice.* A muffled voice, with no resonance and little carrying power, comes from the habit of speaking without much movement of the lower jaw. The remedy is to move the jaw freely as you speak. Exercise it at home, in the bath tub, in bed, or while driving to work. Open the jaw wide; stretch the muscles. Then open and close it rapidly. Wag the jaw from side to side. Get the jaw and the facial muscles thoroughly limbered up. Your speaking voice will quickly improve.

4. *Nervousness.* Many vocal problems, including reediness, shrillness, shortness of breath and lack of power, may be caused by nervousness. The speaker has a good conversational voice, but loses it when he gets on the platform. Work at developing self-confidence as suggested in Chapter 8, and these problems will clear up by themselves.

Posture

Correct posture improves your voice. Stand erect. Don't let your head bow forward or sink down between the shoulders: bending or shortening of the neck muffles the voice.

Your chest, shoulders, neck, jaw and face should be relaxed. If you have the opportunity, loosen these muscles before going on the platform. Stretch the arms and shrug the shoulders. Roll your head round a few times slowly: let it hang forward, then tilt it on to the right shoulder, let it hang back, then tilt to the left shoulder, then forward again. After a few times round, reverse direction. Don't do it too fast or too often; you may make yourself dizzy or nauseated. Yawn several times, give a broad smile and take several deep, sighing breaths. (Of course, don't do these exercises where the audience can see you!)

Note the relaxed feeling that follows the exercises. Eventually you will find you can produce the relaxation without the exercises, just by willing it.

Developing Power

Public speaking needs more power than conversation. There are two ways to get that power.

The wrong way is to force air violently past the vocal cords: that is, to shout. This gives ample power, but it tires you, and soon causes hoarseness and temporary loss of voice. If you persist in shouting, you will in time become permanently hoarse. So don't shout!

The right way is to *project*; that is, to make full use of the resonating cavities of the chest, mouth and head. This gives power without shouting. Here are some hints on projecting.

Imagine you are going to move your voice out of your throat and put it immediately behind your front teeth.

First, with the voice in the throat, say aloud, "My voice is deep, deep down in the back of my throat."

Feel the vibration in your throat.

Now, move the voice up and forward and say aloud, "Now the voice is high and forward, just behind my front teeth."

There is no need to go into the anatomy of projection. The forward placement of the voice comes quite easily if you simply *think* about bringing it forward.

Some people find it helpful to think of the voice being produced by a tiny loudspeaker at the front of the mouth. Others think of the voice emerging from a little ball of light just behind the front teeth.

However you imagine it, think of placing the voice forward like this, and your voice will at once become clearer and more powerful. This is what we call "projecting."

Here is an exercise in projection. Hum on an "m" sound, fairly loudly. There should be no feeling of vibration in the throat, but a strong vibration in the lips and in the roots of the front teeth. After humming for a while to get the feel of it, open the lips and recite

The moan of doves in immemorial elms,
The murmur of innumerable bees.

Hum again, and then say, "Speak the speech, I pray you, trippingly on the tongue. Let the sound come out; move your jaw and open your mouth wider than in private conversation."

Check yourself as you deliver a speech. If there is any strain or vibration in the throat, you are not projecting, so think again of bringing the voice forward. Then the vibration, if any, will be felt in your mouth and head.

There is nothing mysterious or difficult about projecting. Babies project as soon as they are born. A baby can scream for hours without getting a sore throat. Most young children project naturally. I have seen children walking to meet the school bus in the mornings; I have heard their voices two hundred yards away, and they were not shouting.

But as they grow up, many people lose the habit of projecting. Boys are in a hurry to develop a deep, manly voice. At puberty they force their voices back as far down their throats as they can. Girls are taught to develop a quiet, muffled voice. So most of us, in order to become powerful speakers, must learn again what we once did naturally.

A few people, although they have no organic defect, find they cannot speak loudly even when they project, because they have such a strongly established habit of speaking softly. The cure is to speak just ten percent louder all the time, in everyday life, for one week. No one will notice the slight change; no one will criticize. Then increase ten percent more the next week, and so on, until the desired power is attained.

Projection is the key to power in public speaking. If you project, you can speak for two hours without tiring or getting hoarse; you can speak clearly even if you have a cold; you can address three thousand people without using a microphone, and make yourself heard even by the deaf lady in the back row.

Articulation

Articulation is the act of speaking so that every sound is clearly heard. Most people do not articulate properly in conversation, but you must do it in public speaking if you want to make yourself understood.

Form the invariable habit of sounding your t's, d's, p's, b's—in fact, all your consonants. The consonants are the first sounds to be lost as the voice travels over a distance; the first to die away in an acoustically dead room; and the first to be smothered in an echoing room. They are the first sounds lost to people who are getting hard of hearing. And remember, *nearly everyone over twenty-five has some degree of hearing-loss.* So hit all consonants hard, especially those at the ends of your words. *Exaggerate* the consonants.

If you ordinarily have the habit of slurring your speech, you will feel somewhat affected when you begin to articulate properly on the platform. Don't worry. Well-articulated speech does not sound affected to an audience; it sounds pleasantly clear. It makes you stand out from the ordinary run of speakers. If you articulate clearly, you will find that people—especially elderly people—come up to you after your speeches and say, "Mr. So-and-so, I heard every word you said!" That is obviously a rare treat for them, and it will be gratifying for you.

Another point is that as you articulate, you automatically move your lips and jaws vigorously. Many people, suffering a slow, unnoticed hearing loss, teach themselves to lip read without knowing it. Those people will easily understand you when you articulate well.

Lastly, perfect articulation means that you need less power; you save your breath, save your strength, and can speak longer, and more easily.

Pitch

Use a medium pitch, not too high, not too low. Most women, in conversation, use a high pitch; they should lower their pitch for public speaking. Men with deep voices should use a higher pitch on the platform.

Variety

To make your voice sound interesting, continually vary the three P's—*Pace, Pitch* and *Power*. Vocal monotony bores listeners; vocal variety keeps them alert. One warning—beware of the variety that turns into monotony. Some speakers, seeking variety of pitch, begin every sentence at a high pitch and run down to the end. This soon produces boredom.

Here again, as you vary the three P's, you may at first feel affected, because you are not used to doing it in conversation. Don't worry; it does not sound affected on the platform. To the audience it sounds interesting and pleasing.

You can also achieve a variety of tone—harsh, sweet, stern, tender, and so on. You need no technical studies to do this. Simply let yourself feel the appropriate emotion, and your voice will automatically take on the tone to express it.

To feel, as you speak, it is only necessary to think as you speak. This is another argument against memorizing or reading your speeches.

When your voice expresses feeling, you will find that the audience reacts emotionally to you and your speech. This heightens your power to persuade and to move them.

As an exercise in tonal variety, put on a long, solemn face and say aloud, "Words alone cannot express my feelings on this occasion."

Now smile and say the same sentence. Notice the difference.

Don't feel that, by consciously controlling your voice, you are being tricky or insincere. Be as sincere as you can! (The audience soon detects insincerity, anyway.) The more sincere you are, in fact, the more deeply you think and the more keenly you feel, the more varied and interesting your voice will be.

General Vocal Development

If you have time, join an amateur drama group and learn to act; it will make you a better speaker. Learn to sing; it will help you control and develop your voice. If you have defective teeth, get them repaired, or have dentures fitted.

Listen to your voice on a good tape recorder. Analyze it honestly. What do you like about it? What do you dislike? Work to develop the features you like and to correct those you dislike.

Remember, you get the kind of voice you deserve, because you get the kind of voice you work for.

Summary

A good voice is simply a good habit.
Don't make non-verbal noises during pauses.
Develop self-confidence; it will improve your voice.
Good posture and muscular relaxation improve your voice.
To make yourself heard easily—project.
To make yourself understood—articulate.
Use a variety of pace, pitch, power and tone.
Work persistently for vocal development.

Exercises

1. Stand before a mirror. Check that your posture is correct. Speak for a few minutes with exaggerated movement of the jaw and face. Really make faces as you speak! This helps to loosen up all the muscles of the face. Repeat from time to time.

2. An exercise in articulation. Read the following sentences aloud, making tongue, jaw and lips move vigorously so that every sound is clearly produced.

Three giant skyscrapers rocked by earth shocks.
Check cotton kerchief red-hot clue to killer.

Dead waiter's diary produced in criminal court.
Eight tots buried under heaps of red sand.
Thousand turkey-cocks believed killed in landslide.
Historic landmark toppled by overloaded sightseers' bus.
Twenty thousand immigrants expected today at dockside.
Scotland and England isolated as quakes rock island.
Canton stays quiet as street riots subside.
Paper stocks dip as pulp operatives' strike spreads.

3. Find in a book, magazine or newspaper, a passage that, for you, could arouse some emotional response—mirth, shame, hatred, etc. First read it casually and unemotionally, listening to the tone of your voice. Then, for one minute, dwell on the emotional content of the passage. Think of what it means. *Make yourself feel* the emotion. Now read the passage again, listening for the change of tone that comes with emotion. Repeat from time to time, as an aid to cultivating a varied, expressive voice.

11. Emphasis and Expression

Speech finely framed delighteth the ears.
2 Maccabees, 15:39

Demosthenes was once asked, "What are the three most important points of oratory?"

He replied, "Action, action and action," meaning that the words you say are less important than the way you say them. The combined action of voice, face, body and arms gives life and power to a speech that would seem dull in print.

Never forget the vast difference between spoken and written communication. If you want to emphasize a word or a phrase in a book, you can set it in *italics* or CAPITALS. But in speaking, you have no typographical aids. So in this chapter we discuss methods for adding emphasis and expression to what you say.

Functions of Emphasis and Expression

1. Emphasis and expression help you attain *clarity*; ensure that there is no mistake about the meaning of what you say. For example, take the sentence, "I want you to give me the knife." Depending on the way you apply emphasis, you can make it mean several different things.

I want you to give me the knife. (i.e., An answer to the question, "Who wants me to give him the knife?")

I want *you* to give me the knife. (i.e., I don't want anyone else to give it to me.)

119

I want you to *give* me the knife. (i.e., I don't expect to pay for it.)

I want you to give *me* the knife. (i.e., Don't give it to Tom, Dick or Harry.)

I want you to give me the *knife.* (i.e., Don't give me a fork or a spoon.)

Sometimes the meaning of a sentence depends on emphasis and expression in ways too subtle to be represented in print. For example, "Every member of this organization knows what has been achieved under the presidency of Mr. Steadfast" can be a tribute to Steadfast, or a condemnation of him, depending on the way the speaker says it, and the way he looks as he says it.

2. Emphasis and expression *heighten interest.* A speech delivered without emphasis or expression will bore your listeners, and so will not achieve your purpose.

Let us look at the means we can use to achieve these two important aims.

Phrasing

From reading, we are accustomed to think of words as the primary units of language, because that is the way they are printed. All the letters composing one word stand close together, and a gap separates that word from adjacent words. Larger language-units in print are sentences and paragraphs, marked off by semicolons, colons, periods and indentations.

In speech the word, sentence and paragraph disappear as units; their place is taken by *the phrase.* The phrase is not a unit of grammar, but *a unit of significance.* Each phrase contains one idea, or one important component of an idea. Within each phrase, as you speak, the words run together into an unbroken stream of sound. Separating each phrase from the next is a pause.

Take the first paragraph under this heading. Let us represent in print the way it would actually be spoken on the platform. Virgules (/) will indicate the pauses that mark the phrase-endings.

Fromreading / weareaccustomedtothinkofwords / astheprimaryunitsoflanguage / becausethatisthewaytheyareprinted /

alltheletterscomposingoneword / standclosetogether / andagap /
separatesthatword / fromadjacentwords /
largerlanguageunitsinprint /
aresentences / andparagraphs / markedoffbysemicolons / colons /
periods / andindentations /

Here is another example:

Fourscoreandsevenyearsago /
ourfathersbroughtforthonthiscontinent / anewnation /
conceivedinliberty / anddedicatedtotheproposition /
thatallmen / arecreatedequal /

Usually there are several possible ways to phrase a passage.
The bigger the audience, the more finely should the ideas be broken
down into components, one component forming each phrase. The
finer breakdown introduces more pauses, reduces the number of
words spoken per minute, and so gives the audience more time to
think. The bigger the audience, the slower it is to absorb ideas.

This example shows two different phrasings. In ordinary print
it is: "The future policy of this organization will be decided, not
by outsiders, but by you, its members and associates, assembled
here in this hall tonight."

Phrasing for a Small Audience.

Thefuturepolicyofthisorganization /
willbedecidednotbyoutsiders / butbyyou /
itsmembersandassociates / assembledhere / inthishalltonight /

Phrasing for a Big Audience.

Thefuturepolicy / ofthisorganization / willbedecided / not /
byoutsiders / butbyyou / itsmembers / andassociates /
assembledhere / inthishall / tonight /

The speech, then, is divided into phrases, each phrase being a
unit of significance. But within each phrase, not all the words are
of equal importance. So to guide the listener's attention, you stress
the most important word or words of each phrase. The stress can
consist of:

1. *A change of power.* Usually there is an increase of volume,

although occasionally a sudden, brief, reduction of volume can effectively stress a word.

2. *A change of pitch.* The word to be stressed is spoken at a higher or lower pitch than the rest of the phrase.

3. *A change of pace.* The unimportant words are spoken rapidly, and the important word is spoken somewhat more slowly, by prolonging its principal vowel sound.

Here is the previous example, spaced out in phrases, with the stressed words in italics:

The*futurepolicy* / of*thisorganization* / willbe*decided* / *not* / by*outsiders* / butby*you* / its*members* / and*associates* / assembled*here* / in*thishall* / *tonight* /

The weight of the thought within each phrase determines the stress on its principal words; the weightier the thought, the heavier the stress. It determines the length of the pause that follows the phrase—the weightier the thought, the longer the pause.

In the preceding example, the phrase / butby*you* / is obviously the most important; so "*you*" will receive a heavier stress than any other word, and the pause following this phrase will be longer than any other pause in the example.

Well-marked phrasing, with appropriate stress on the key words of each phrase, leads the audience effortlessly through your speech. *It forces the audience to understand.*

Moreover, phrasing gives a pleasing variety to the speech because:

(1) The phrases are of different lengths; they produce a constantly varying rhythm that makes the speech sound interesting.

(2) The different degrees of stress produce a pattern of pitch, pace and power variations that is superimposed on the basic phrase-rhythm.

(3) The pauses of different lengths give a third rhythm, of silent periods.

Some beginning speakers neglect phrasing, because they are in such a hurry to say what is on their minds. Some are reluctant to pause; they fear that the audience will think they are at a loss for words. You do, in fact, use the pause after one phrase to find and arrange the words for your next phrase. But the listeners do not know or care what you are doing during the pause. All they are concerned with is that the pause gives *them* time to think.

Of course, if you put on an anxious expression, writhe about, and look desperately out the window or up at the ceiling during pauses, the audience knows you are scrambling for ideas and words. So, keep a calm expression on your face, keep looking steadily at the audience, and take all the time you need to think.

The brighter members of the audience derive a special pleasure from these pauses. During the few moments of silence, such listeners think ahead, trying to anticipate your next phrase. Whether they are right or wrong, they enjoy the mental exercise, and their concentration on you and your message is intensified.

Facial Expression

The audience judges you and your speech not only by your voice, but also by each expression that moves across your face. The best results will follow if your facial expression changes to suit the sense of what you are saying at each moment.

A fixed expression of anxiety is common with beginners; they are concentrating on finding the right words, and delivering them clearly. This facial immobility is excusable in early practice sessions, so long as it does not develop into a habit.

Some experienced speakers have a poker-faced delivery, perhaps because nobody has ever told them how dull it looks. Poker-faced speaking not only looks monotonous but it also sounds monotonous. A fixed facial expression produces an unvarying tone of voice.

One speaker told me he maintained a poker face deliberately, because he felt that to change his expression would be insincere. Such a speaker could vary his expression effectively and sincerely, if he accustomed himself to *feeling,* as well as thinking, on the platform.

There is no need to learn facial expressions from a chart, no need to consider which expression to wear at which moment. Simply put some emotion into your speaking—*make yourself feel.* Look after the feeling, and the face will look after itself!

Some people's faces are stiff and unexpressive through lack of practice in registering emotion. These exercises will relieve that stiffness.

1. Practice feeling and showing emotion off the platform, in everyday life. Begin by making yourself smile at least five times a day (when the occasion is appropriate, of course.)

2. When smiling feels easy and natural, go on to other expressions—surprise, sadness, puzzlement, doubt, suspicion, and so on. I repeat: there is no need consciously to shape and rehearse an expression. Simply make yourself feel, and let your face do what comes naturally.

3. Limber up your facial muscles by several daily sessions of wide yawning, followed by pulling funny faces. (This is best done in private.)

4. Immediately before going on to the platform to speak, do the relaxation of exercises described in Chapter 10 (p. 117). They relieve tension in the muscles of face and neck, help the face to be more expressive and, as a bonus, help to improve the tone and resonance of your voice.

Gesture

As we have seen, if you *feel* as you speak, your face will convey your feelings to the audience. Your arms and body, if you let them, will do the same thing, and will help to make the audience share your feelings. In a big hall, gesture helps you to reach and to move the people who are sitting too far away to see your face clearly.

In some parts of the world people gesture vigorously in conversation. Here, women do gesture to some extent as they speak; men gesture seldom or not at all. This, however, gives women no advantage. The small, fluttering gestures that women use are ineffective on the platform. For public speaking, women and men alike must acquire new habits of using their hands, arms and bodies.

Effective gesturing is usually the last thing a speaker learns to do. Some never learn it at all. I recently saw a middle-aged politician, a veteran of many platform appearances, trying to gesture. His favorite move was to bend his elbow at right angles and hold the forearm stiffly across his chest. Keeping the arm in this position for minutes at a time, he would emphasize various points by wagging his hand from the wrist!

There is no need to slip into such habits as that. Here is a program that will lead you on to gesturing confidently and effectively:

1. Don't try to gesture at all in your first few practice speeches. Just get used to thinking and speaking on your feet while facing the audience. Meanwhile establish a few acceptable, basic, hand positions.

At first, in this non-gesturing period, you may find that your hands feel big and conspicuous. You think that the audience is staring at your hands. (Beginning actors have this feeling, too.)

So here are some suggestions on what to do with your hands.

a) If you are not holding notes, let your hands hang at your sides. Don't clench the fists; don't force the fingers out straight; don't straighten the elbows into a military "attention" position. All arm and hand muscles should be relaxed, then the elbows and fingers will be slightly, naturally, flexed.

b) A woman can clasp her hands lightly together in front of her body. (This looks awkward for a man.)

c) On informal occasions—say for after-dinner speeches—a man can place one hand in his trousers pocket and let the other hang loose.

d) For informal occasions it is also appropriate for a man to place both hands in the jacket pockets.

e) Don't clasp your hands behind your back. It looks awkward for men and women. Moreover, you are tempted to tighten the clasp more and more, until you produce an unpleasant, tiring, tension in your arms.

f) At a table, you can rest your hands lightly on top of it, so long as you don't have to stoop. At a lectern, you can lightly grasp the sloping surface that supports the papers. Don't *lean* on a table; don't *cling* to a lectern.

g) If you are holding your notes, grasp them in one hand and let other hang at your side.

Continue speaking without gesturing until you find you are no longer conscious of your hands.

2. When you can speak with some freedom and fluency, begin to put more and more feeling into your speeches. Make your face express your feelings. Still do not force yourself to gesture.

3. When your face has become expressive, start to think to yourself, "Now I will begin to use gestures."

There is no need to plan and rehearse the gestures you will make. By now you can relax on the platform; by now you feel fairly confident as you speak. So just continue to intensify your feelings; continue to tell yourself, "When I feel like gesturing, *I'll do it without thinking.*"

Suddenly you find that, without planning, with perfect self-confidence, you are beginning to use gestures. When the words, voice and feeling, are developed, and when the desire to gesture is present, the gestures follow automatically.

4. Now, when you find yourself gesturing spontaneously, give some thought to developing your gestures, so that they have the best possible effect on the audience.

a) Never use meaningless, unfeeling gestures. You will not do that if you follow the program of development described above. But if you have practiced gestures separately, you may be tempted to throw them in at various spots where they are not needed. Never gesture unless you feel you must!

b) Use *few* gestures. A gesture is a means of emphasizing an idea. But constant emphasis is no emphasis.

c) Make your gestures broad. Don't flap a hand on the wrist-joint while keeping the rest of the arm motionless. Never hold your elbows at your sides and try to gesture with forearms only. Every gesture should be made with the whole arm moving freely at shoulder, elbow and wrist. And the bigger the audience, the bigger must be the gestures.

d) Gesture *on the word* that you wish to emphasize—not before it, not after it, but exactly on the word. There is one exception to this rule. If you are going to hammer with your fist on table or lectern, then hammer a fraction of a second after the word. Hammering on the word will prevent the audience from hearing the word.

e) Sustain the gesture for some time. It looks ridiculous to shoot your arm out and immediately pull it back as if you had touched a hot stove. Normally, an idea that is important enough to merit a gesture is important enough to be followed by a long pause. Hold the gesture throughout the pause. If, as sometimes happens, the idea and gesture produce applause, hold the gesture for several seconds, then lower the arm slowly. A quick movement of the arm would choke off the applause prematurely.

f) Let your eye follow the gesture. If you point upward, to

the right or to the left, look where you point, but only briefly. Let your gaze return to the audience almost at once.

g) Move not only the hands and arms, but also the whole body. Let the body lean slightly in the direction the arm is moving. If you are not pinned down by a lectern or microphone, move one of your feet slightly in the same direction.

h) Carefully observe how other people use gestures. Watch experienced and inexperienced speakers; see which movements look strong and effective, and which look weak and meaningless. Imitate good gestures and avoid bad ones.

Eye Contact

I have mentioned elsewhere that good eye contact between speaker and audience is a powerful aid to communication. So, except for the moments when you glance at your notes, keep your eyes moving over the audience. Don't gaze fixedly at one part of the audience—say at a group of your friends, or at a very important person.

Keep looking into the eyes of the audience. This not only helps to convey your feelings to them, it allows you to see, by their expressions, how they are reacting to your speech.

Summary

What you say is less important that how you say it.
Emphasis and expression give clarity and maintain interest.
Each phrase is a unit of significance.
The phrases are separated by pauses.
The bigger the audience, the shorter the phrases.
Stress the important word or words of each phrase.
Phrasing gives variety to your speech.
Facial expressions help to convey your meaning.
Gestures help the audience to share your feelings.
Gestures should be few and broad.
Gesture on the word you wish to emphasize.
Maintain eye contact with the audience.

Exercises

Here is an excerpt from one of Abraham Lincoln's speeches.

What constitutes the bulwark of our own liberty and independence? It is not our frowning battlements, our bristling sea coasts, our army and our navy. These are not our reliance against tyranny. All of those may be turned against us without making us weaker for the struggle. Our reliance is in the love of liberty which God has planted in us. Our defense is in the spirit which prized liberty as the heritage of all men in all lands everywhere. Destroy this spirit and you have planted the seeds of despotism at your own doors. Familiarize yourselves with the chains of bondage and you prepare your own limbs to wear them. Accustomed to trample on the rights of others, you have lost the genius of your own independence and become the fit subjects of the first cunning tyrant who rises among you.

Copy this script. Mark it off into phrases, and underline in each phrase the word or words to stress:

1. For an audience of 50
2. For an audience of 1,000

Practice reading the speech at appropriate speeds for each audience. Think what it means. Make yourself *feel* the relevant emotions, and produce the appropriate facial expressions and gestures.

12. The Speaker-Audience Relationship

It takes two to speak the truth—one to speak and another to hear.

HENRY DAVID THOREAU

Without an audience, you cannot deliver a speech; you can only rehearse. And, as everyone knows who has made a speech, speaking is vastly different from rehearsing.

As soon as a speaker faces an audience, an emotional force flows between him and his listeners. That force is powerful; it can send them into fits of laughter, spur them to destructive rage, make them shed tears of pity or, misused, send them off to sleep. Passing from auditorium to platform, that emotional force can reduce an inexperienced speaker to temporary dumbness; it can stimulate a confident speaker to unaccustomed heights of eloquence.

Let us examine the qualities of the audience and see how they affect the speaker-audience relationship.

Number

The audience consists of a number of people, more or less closely packed together. Consequently its members no longer think and act as individuals. They not only react to the speaker; they also act upon each other.

1. In an audience, emotions are infectious. Edward Gibbon describes this phenomenon:

The coldest nature is animated, the firmest reason is moved, by the rapid communication of the prevailing impulse; and each hearer

129

is affected by his own passion and by those of the surrounding multitude.

So it is easier to move an audience than to move most individuals, to mirth, love, fear, hatred, or any other emotion. Your words, looks and gestures can impress, easily and quickly, the few most susceptible listeners. Their emotion can be communicated to those around them, and soon affect everyone.

This is why a claque, a few people paid to applaud, is effective in the theater. The commercial enthusiasm of the claqueurs infects the rest of the audience, and makes the performance a success.

This spreading of emotion through the audience can facilitate your speaking—can do much of your work for you. But, if you are not careful, it can work against you, because boredom, doubt and puzzlement can spread through an audience just as easily as the more desirable emotions. So you dare not neglect the deaf lady in the back row, lest she form the nucleus of a spreading area of dissatisfaction and hostility. So you make every effort to carry *all* the audience along with you *all* the time.

By the same process of infection, the emotion of the audience gives back to the speaker an emotional impulse many times stronger than the original impulse that he directed toward the audience. When a speech is going well, the speaker stimulates the audience, and the audience stimulates the speaker. It is a thrilling sensation for the speaker. Be prepared for it; work toward it; and, when it comes to you, enjoy it.

2. The reactions of an audience are *slower* than those of one or two people. The transmission of emotion is not instantaneous, and the bigger the audience, the more time it takes.

The reactions of a large audience are slow to begin and slow to die away. This is one reason for speaking slowly (another is the acoustic quality of a large building). Only when the slowest thinking listener understands, can you fairly say that the audience understands. So you go at such a pace that the slowpokes can keep up with you.

Fortunately for speakers, the quick-thinking listeners do not resent this deliberation. Once you have the whole audience thinking and feeling in unison, they will want to keep moving together along the course of your argument.

3. The reactions of an audience are *more intense* than those of one or a few people. For example, in conversation you make a witticism that elicits a chuckle from your listeners. Deliver the same witticism successfully to a big audience, and you may win a roar of laughter.

This is a further effect of emotional infection. The reaction of *the most susceptible* listener becomes the model for the reactions of all the others.

The same applies to other emotional reactions—pride, shame, desire, and so on. Remarks which might move an individual to say, ''Too bad! Something should be done about that!'' can move a crowd to riot, burn and kill.

4. These effects, then, depend on the number of listeners, and the greater that number, the more marked will these effects be. They also depend on the degree to which the listeners are crowded together. A hundred people seated in an unbroken block will react more slowly and more intensely than the same hundred scattered thinly about a hall.

You can use this knowledge to help you control your audience. For the maximum emotional effect, get the audience together. (See Chapter 20 for means of doing this.) But, if the audience is hostile to you, you will obviously want to minimize their emotional reactions; so leave them scattered apart.

Diversity

The audience is a group of people who meet for a common purpose, but who are usually diverse in age, sex, intelligence, prejudices, politics, religion, occupations, economic circumstances, and knowledge of the subject. There is no such thing as a homogeneous audience; there are only audiences less or more diverse.

Speaking to one person whom you know well, you can easily frame your remarks so that they appeal strongly to him. But how are you to reach the minds and hearts of a widely assorted crowd of people, most of whom you do not know at all? And remember, you must reach those minds and hearts *quickly,* before any of them has time to feel bored.

1. *Simplify.* Complex arguments and subtle distinctions **are**

lost on the audience, just as tiny gestures are imperceptible and faint sounds are inaudible to them. A good speech consists of *a few clear points,* well hammered home.

2. *Unify.* Begin at a point of agreement; get the audience thinking and feeling in unison from your first sentence.

3. *Moderate pace.* Speak at a moderate pace, and deal with your material at a moderate pace, to allow ample time for each phrase and idea to be understood.

4. *Repeat.* Never be afraid of repeating a word or an idea. Repeat each point in different ways, with different illustrations and proofs, so that it is fully consolidated before you move on. Occasionally review the ground you have already covered. Do this several times during the body of a long speech; do it in the conclusion of long and short speeches.

To sum up this point: the speaker's task is, as far as possible, *to unify the diversified,* to offer them material they can all understand, presented in a way they can all accept.

Concentration

An audience cannot concentrate long on one point. The listeners' power to absorb new information rises fairly rapidly at first, as they become more interested in the subject, but levels off after fifteen minutes, and declines sharply after thirty minutes. After fifty minutes, they are absorbing almost nothing. In the last five minutes of an hour-long speech—if they know the end is near—the listeners' power of absorption increases again.

However, the audience can be refreshed at any point, and its power of absorption renewed, by arranging some change of activity—that is, a change from sitting and listening.

The most efficient arrangement for an hour-long session is what might be called the layer-cake format:

15 minutes—speech
5 minutes—questions and discussion
15 minutes—speech
5 minutes—questions and discussion
15 minutes—speech
5 minutes—questions and discussion

If you can choose your own format, consider using this one. But often you have to speak straight through your time-allowance. A straight fifteen-minute speech presents no difficulties on this point. But if you have to make a long, uninterrupted speech, give it all the variety you can.

Make prominent division between the various points as you cover them. As each point is finished with, say something to this effect: "So much for that. Now let's move on and look at something else."

Make a noticeable pause, and begin again at a different pitch, with a different tone of voice, and at a different pace. This will have some effect in restoring the audience's power to concentrate, absorb and remember.

Credulity

All audiences are basically conservative—that is, they want to hear their own opinions confirmed. If you do not agree with their opinions, they at least want you to discuss them sympathetically and politely.

It used to be said that young people were more credulous than older ones. I doubt whether this is true any longer. I was recently told that children now disbelieve eighty percent of what they see and hear on TV. So it may be that the old are now more credulous than the young.

Anyway, it is well to be on the safe side, and to assume that the audience does not necessarily believe anything just because you say it. But you can improve your prospects of being believed. Here are ten ways to inspire confidence; ten things that will make audiences more willing to trust you.

1. Your appearance should be generally attractive, and your clothes appropriate for the occasion. Signs of bodily neglect—excess weight, poor posture, unhealthy complexion, dandruff, decaying or dirty teeth—lead some people to think, "He is careless about his own body, so he must be careless about everything else." This may not be fair, but it is the way many people feel. So let your appearance speak in your favor.

2. Cultivate, and use on the platform, a frank, open manner. Good eye contact tends to inspire confidence. It is a common belief that the man who looks you in the eye must be telling the truth. The

notion is unfounded but, as a speaker, you dare not ignore it. (Another reason for not reading speeches!) Come to the point quickly. When listeners begin thinking, ''What's he driving at?'' they tend to wonder whether you are being frank with them.

3. A moderate pace inspires confidence. The fast talker is automatically suspect. ''He's rushing me,'' says the listener to himself. ''He won't give me time to think.''

Illogical as it may sound, the slow speaker tends to be trusted.

4. Avoid personal abuse of people present or absent. It may get a laugh, but it alienates some of your audience, and makes them feel you are unprincipled.

5. Be credible in what you say. Don't exaggerate; don't make unsupported statements. Bring forward evidence, examples, statistics, to prove your points.

6. Answer questions fully, politely and frankly.

7. Be punctual. Lateness irritates and alienates listeners and the organizers of meetings. ''If he can't be trusted to tell the time, he can't be trusted in anything!''

8. Be reliable. Fulfill promises to the letter. Such conduct builds for you an exceptional reputation. You acquire scarcity-value, because there are not many completely reliable people around.

9. Be prepared. If you have to admit, ''I don't really know what I'm going to say tonight,'' how can you expect the audience to feel any confidence in you?

10. Develop self-confidence. If you doubt yourself, the audience is not likely to trust you. But a serene, imperturbable self-confidence is communicated to the audience, and tends to give them confidence in you and in what you say.

Sensitivity

Listeners soon become irritated if they feel that you are bullying, insulting or patronizing them. Here again, emotion is quickly transmitted from the few most sensitive listeners to the others. So take care not to excite their sensitivity.

Don't make direct attacks on the opinions of the audience. Don't put forward your opinions in an aggressive, unpleasant way.

You'll be making a very foolish mistake if you vote for my opponent.

This idea of a new swimming pool is completely misguided: it's ridiculous to suggest such a thing. The only sensible course is to continue as we are, with the old pool.

I've investigated it thoroughly, and I can tell you you're crazy if you miss the opportunity to sign up for the charter flight with ABC airline. Those people who are gabbing about the XYZ charter just don't understand the travel business.

This sort of talk will arouse opposition instead of winning agreement.

Feelings for the Speaker

We saw earlier that an audience will not remain neutral toward the subject of your speech; they will react emotionally toward it, either favorably or unfavorably.

Neither will they remain neutral toward you, the speaker. They will quickly develop a set of emotional reactions—goodwill or hostility, trust or distrust, respect or scorn.

For a successful speech, then, it is not enough to speak your words clearly and with due emphasis; you also need to win the goodwill of the audience. The quickest and surest way to do that is to feel goodwill toward your audience. If necessary, deliberately cultivate this goodwill. Here is a method that works.

1. Prepare yourself mentally, by *thinking* favorably about the audience and what you are going to say to them.

I am interested in these people, I'll give them my very best. I believe they will be interested in me, and in my subject, and in what I say about it.

Frame such thoughts; hold them in your mind; repeat them often. You will find that your feeling toward the speaking engagement and toward the audience will improve.

2. Motivate yourself. *Write down* reasons why you want to give of your best, why you want to succeed, and to win the respect and goodwill of this audience.

3. *Talk favorably* in advance about the occasion, the speech, and the audience.

4. *Smile* as you mount the platform and face the audience. As you *look* pleased, you will tend to *feel* pleased, and the audience will tend to feel favorably toward you.

Will Rogers became an exceptionally popular speaker, although he was lacking in orthodox public speaking technique. His success was largely based on the warm, friendly relationship he established and maintained with his audiences. The secret is revealed in his remark, ''I never met a man I didn't like.''

Resolve to like your audience. *Make* yourself like them, and you will find that they tend to like you. This favorable emotional interchange will make speaking easier for you, and listening more enjoyable for them.

Summary

There is an emotional interchange between speaker and audience.

In an audience, emotions are infectious.

Audience reactions are slower than those of individuals.

Audience reactions are stronger than those of individuals.

The bigger the audience, the stronger its reactions.

The audience is diverse.

To communicate effectively:

1. Simplify. Make a few clear points.
2. Unify. Begin at a point of agreement.
3. Proceed at a moderate pace.
4. Repeat each point in different ways.

Varied presentation helps listeners absorb your material.

Try to win the confidence of the audience.

Try to win the goodwill of the audience.

Feel and show goodwill toward your audience.

Exercises

These exercises will give you a thorough knowledge of the speaker-audience relationship. Repeat them as often as you like.

1. Take an opportunity to listen to a good speaker. Don't let

yourself get absorbed in the subject matter of his speech; don't surrender to the emotions he arouses in the audience. Have pen and notebook handy, and analyze for your own instruction what he does, and its effect on the audience. As you repeat the exercise, you will find you can detect the precise technical means that speakers use to produce specific results.

2. If you happen to hear a bad speaker, don't just sit there feeling bored. Get out the pen and notebook. Record the things that he does wrong, and their effect on the audience.

13. Language for the Speaker

Pregnant in matter, in expression brief,
Let every sentence stand with bold relief. . . .
Nor deal with pompous phrase, nor e'er suppose
Poetic flights belong to reasoning prose.

JOSEPH STORY

Your task is to convey ideas from your mind to the minds of your listeners. Ideas are non-verbal; for many people they are wholly pictorial. For example, you have a clear idea of the chair you are sitting on. But how would you describe it *in words* to an audience of Martians who had never seen a chair?

You have a good idea of what an election is. But try describing it in words!

In private speech you don't do much of this exposition. Most of the people you talk to know what you are talking about. They are members of your family, club or church; they are friends or fellow-workers. You share with them a common stock of ideas.

But in public speaking you cannot assume that everyone in the audience shares your stock of ideas. You will often have to explain those ideas, in order to make the audience understand.

For example, suppose that in a political speech, you talk about justice, and a questioner says, "Mr. Speaker, please explain exactly what you mean by justice."

Or suppose you have to explain democracy, mortality, the gold standard, the union shop, the shape of a spiral staircase, or the thrill of water skiing, to an audience that knows nothing of those things.

Words are your tools, and you will need to choose your words, say them and arrange them, to best effect.

Vocabulary

A speaker short of words is like a soldier short of ammunition. So enlarge your vocabulary. Read with the collector's eye, seeking new words. Consult the dictionary for their pronunciation and meaning. Write them in a notebook and review the list regularly. Listen with the collector's ear to radio, TV, movies, conversation and speeches. Similarly check, note and learn the new words.

Check your present vocabulary for wrong meanings and mispronunciations. Do you pronounce some words differently from other people? Then find who is right.

Correct pronunciation is important to you as a speaker; errors undermine your authority. If listeners hear you say "artic" for "arctic" "indentification" for "identification," or "Eye-talian" for "Italian," and so on, they think, "This speaker is careless and wrong about the simple matter of pronunciation; probably he is careless about the evidence he quotes, and wrong about the conclusions he draws."

People distrust a surgeon with dirty hands or a carpenter with blunt tools. Listeners distrust the speaker who does not know how to use words.

Pronunciation of some words varies from region to region. In such cases, be natural; use your native accent unless it is so thick and strange that it would puzzle your hearers. If so, you will have to modify it—cultivate something of a neutral, non-regional accent. You can easily do this with a tape recorder and a little patience.

Style

Your style is the characteristic manner in which you arrange your words and sentences. Here are some qualities that make a good speaking style.

Clarity

The reader can look back at a line if he fails to understand it, can pause and think about it until the meaning is clear. Your listeners cannot do that. Your voice continues, delivering more and more material. If a listener pauses to think over one sentence, he misses the next.

So you cannot afford to puzzle any of your listeners. Every idea must be made clear before you move on to discuss another idea.

So avoid foreign words and uncommon words that some listeners might not understand. If you use abbreviations, e.g., C.A.A., D.O.T., etc, explain them.

Repetition of words or phrases can be a great aid to clarity. William Pitt said, in 1777:

If I were an American, as I am an Englishman, while a foreign troop was landed in my country, I never would lay down my arms— never, never, never!

No listener could be in any doubt about Pitt's views on this subject.

We need a new courthouse now, because the old one has not enough courtrooms. So trials are delayed, prisoners are held in jail longer than they should be, and civil cases drag on long after they should be settled.

We need a new courthouse now, because the fire marshal has condemned the old one, and it would cost more to remodel it than to build a new one.

We need a new courthouse now, because we are going to build a new jail anyway, and we can save nearly a million dollars by putting the two buildings on one site, under one roof.

No listener can fail to understand that we need a new courthouse now.

Simplicity

Repetitions like those quoted above may look out of place on paper. But spoken style is different from literary style. For example, take the speech about the new courthouse. A literary man might express the same idea like this.

Lack of space in the existing courthouse is reported to be causing serious delays in the administration of justice, with accompanying inconvenience to members of the public. The building fails to conform, so competent officials say, to current fire and safety regulations. Moreover, there are obvious possibilities for economy in construction and operation if the custodial and judicial functions of the law can be carried on in the same premises. Weighing these arguments, one concludes that the erection of a new courthouse would be desirable at this time.

Read this aloud. Then read aloud the speech-style version. You will notice that the simpler version sounds better, is more forceful, and is more easily understood.

If you write scripts and read or memorize them, you risk slipping into an obscure, literary style. If you have done a lot of reading and not much speaking, you may find yourself talking like a book, even when speaking from notes. You can avoid that danger by following these suggestions.

1. Use fairly short sentences.

2. Always indicate *promptly* and *prominently* what you are talking about, e.g., "We need a new courthouse" at the beginning and repeated, in the spoken version, instead of "the erection of a new courthouse" mentioned once and tucked away at the end of the literary version.

3. Use specific words instead of abstract ones, e.g., "prisoners are held in jail" instead of "inconvenience to members of the public."

Vividness

Your aim as a speaker is to make your listeners *feel,* to give them a series of emotional experiences. The quickest, surest way to reach the emotions is through the senses. So you will not be content to appeal only to their sense of hearing; you will appeal to sight, touch, smell and taste as well.

Don't say, "Mr. A seems uncertain which party he is supporting." Instead say, "Mr. A is trying to ride two horses at once." You make the audience *see* something.

Aristotle says that a mastery of metaphor is the greatest asset an orator can have. Use metaphors and similes freely. In other words, don't struggle to tell the audience *what it is;* tell them *what it is like.*

Mr. B should never have run for mayor. He has bitten off more than he can chew.

Ye are the salt of the earth; but if the salt have lost its savor, wherewith shall it be salted? It is thenceforth good for nothing but to be cast out and trodden under foot of men (*Jesus of Nazareth*)

He smote the rock of the national resources, and abundant streams of revenue gushed forth. He touched the dead corpse of Public Credit, and it sprung upon its feet. (*Daniel Webster*)

> Sweet are the uses of adversity
> Which, like the toad, ugly and venomous,
> Wears yet a precious jewel in his head.
> (*William Shakespeare*)

Variety

Let your language and your manner of delivery vary from one part of your speech to another, so that it is appropriate to whatever you are discussing. When you are talking about trifles, let language and manner be light; for weighty matters, be serious, for shameful things be scornful, and so on.

Vary the length of your sentences: in emotional passages they should be short; in calm passages they can be longer.

For example, on the "New Courthouse" theme, this would be an appropriate opening:

Eighty-three years ago next month, this city celebrated a public holiday to mark the opening of its new courthouse—the same courthouse that still stands on the east side of our Civic Square.

Speaker and audience are calm at this point, so the sentence can be long and flowing. But for the conclusion, at the climax of the speaker's emotional appeal, and of the audience's emotional response, something like this would be appropriate:

Friends, you have heard the evidence. You know we need a new courthouse. You know we need it *now*. Your votes can give us that courthouse; the referendum is next Monday. I urge you to vote "Yes."

Another good means of creating variety is to stop *telling* the audience about the subject and start *asking* them about it—use what are called rhetorical questions.

What shall it profit a man if he shall gain the whole world and lose his own soul?

Rhetorical questions are unsurpassed as a means of making the audience think, but they can be dangerous. For example, I heard a man speaking against capital punishment. He said, "Is there any man here who would dare to serve as hangman?"

A voice from the audience: "I would!"

Taken aback, the speaker tried to recover. "I think perhaps that when it came to the actual execution day, you wouldn't want to do the job."

The voice, with obvious gusto, said: "You bet I would!"

The speaker's point was destroyed.

So ask only *safe* rhetorical questions, that you know will not draw an unfavorable reply. For example, at a trade-union meeting, you could very well ask, "Is there any man here who would betray the union? Is there any man here who would stab his fellow-workers in the back for the sake of a paltry few dollars and a smile from the boss? Is there any man here who would be a scab?"

Tact

The way you express an idea, as much as the validity of the idea itself, determines its acceptance or rejection by the audience. There are five basic ways of addressing the audience.

1. *"I"*

A personal testimonial is sometimes effective:

"I have tried this course of exercises and I.... etc."

"I was a sinner, and now I am saved."

"I used to have a memory like a sieve and then I took So-and-so's memory-training course, and.... etc."

This first person address is particularly effective if it discloses something slightly to the discredit of the speaker, as in two of the examples above. But beware of using "I" too much, if it seems to imply superior knowledge or intelligence on your part.

"I have studied the matter thoroughly, and I have noticed that. . . . etc."

"I find that. . . . etc."

"I recommend that. . . . etc."

Excessive use of the "I" arouses resentment.

2. *"YOU"*

An appeal to the audience's knowledge or reason is always effective.

"You have probably found that. . . ."

"You will see that. . . ."

"As you already know. . . ."

"You will remember that. . . ."

"As, no doubt, you have noticed. . . ."

Mark Antony said, "I tell you that which you yourselves do know" and, "You all did see. . . . I thrice presented him a kingly crown which he did thrice refuse."

This is the most tactful and most effective way to address the audience. Alexander Pope sums up the technique:

> Men must be taught as if you taught them not,
> And things unknown proposed as things forgot.

It is scarcely possible to overdo the use of the "You" in public speaking. (But the expression "you people" is best avoided—it sounds patronizing.)

3. *"HE, SHE or IT"*

A reference to some third-party authority is usually effective, provided that the audience recognizes that authority.

"Professor X says that. . . ."

"Webster's Dictionary defines it as. . . ."

"Solomon said that. . . ."

"UNESCO reports that. . . ."

4. *"WE"*

Another good form of address involves an appeal to the common knowledge or experience of speaker and audience.

"We have all felt the painful effects of pollution on. . . ."

"We are all taxpayers, and so we all want to. . . ."

"As residents of this city, we all know that. . . ."

5. *"THEY"*

You can cite multiple authorities.

"Eighty-five percent of the population of this country believes that...."

"Every literate person knows that...."

"Common experience indicates that...."

"In this last week, five different people have told me that...."

To sum up this point, then—the most tactful form of language is the direct appeal to the audience's own knowledge or reason; the least tactful is the ostentatious display of the speaker's knowledge.

Summary

The speaker transforms ideas into words.
Develop a copious vocabulary.
Know the meanings of the words you use.
Mispronunciation undermines your authority.
The qualities of a good speaking style are:

1. Clarity
2. Simplicity
3. Vividness
4. Variety

Beware of using "I" too often.
Appeal often to the audience's knowledge: "You know...."
Refer to third-party authorities: "He says...."
Get the audience with you: "We know...."
Cite multiple authorities: "They say...."

Exercises

1. Here is a passage from Edward Gibbon's description of the organization of the Roman army in formal, literary language:

The peasant, or mechanic, imbibed the useful prejudice that he was advanced to the more dignified profession of arms, in which his rank and reputation would depend on his own valour; and that, although the prowess of a private soldier must often escape the notice of fame, his own behaviour might sometimes confer glory or disgrace on the company, the legion, or even the army, to whose honours he was associated. On his first entrance into the service, an oath was administered to him, with every circumstance of solemnity. He promised never to desert his standard, to submit his own will to the commands of his leaders, and to sacrifice his life for the safety of the emperor and the empire. The attachment of the Roman troops to their standards was inspired by the united influence of religion and of honour. The golden eagle, which glittered in the front of the legion, was the object of their fondest devotion; nor was it esteemed less impious than it was ignominious, to abandon that sacred ensign in the hour of danger. These motives, which derived their strength from the imagination, were enforced by fears and hopes of a more substantial kind. Regular pay, occasional donatives, and a stated recompense, after the appointed time of service, alleviated the hardships of the military life, whilst, on the other hand, it was impossible for cowardice or disobedience to escape the severest punishment. The centurions were authorised to chastise with blows, the generals had a right to punish with death; and it was an inflexible maxim of Roman discipline, that a good soldier should dread his own officers far more than the enemy. From such laudable arts did the valour of the Imperial troops receive a degree of firmness and docility unattainable by the impetuous and irregular passions of barbarians.

Read this aloud. Then expound the meaning of it in clear, simple, vivid language of your own choice. Here are some hints on procedure:

    a) Break the passage down into separate ideas.

    b) Write a short note to express each idea.

    c) From the notes, deliver your spoken version.

2. Take some subject that you know well—something connected with job, studies or hobbies, for example—and deliver an explanatory speech about it. Use the ''I'' form of address as little as possible; appeal as often as you can to the audience's own knowledge and experience.

14. On the Platform

Let your speech be always with grace.

COLOSSIANS IV:6

A thoroughly prepared speech, and a good voice to deliver it, will carry you far, but not all the way, to success as a speaker. Here are some hints that will make your platform work easier, more graceful, more pleasing to listeners and more satisfying to you.

Be Prepared

You are going to speak at a meeting of some kind. Ideally, you should be able to concentrate on getting yourself and your notes on to the platform. The chairman should take care of everything else.

But you cannot depend on that. Perhaps the chairman is inexperienced, and does not understand his duties. The man chosen as chairman could have fallen sick, and a substitute may have been appointed at the last minute. You cannot guarantee a supply of experienced, thoughtful chairmen but, if you are prepared, you can smooth over many of the difficulties that arise from inadequate chairmanship.

1. Type out the facts that you would like to have mentioned in an introduction. Hand it to the chairman, or to the person who is to introduce you. This produces better results than a brief conversation during which the introducer jots down a few notes on a scrap of paper.

2. Before the meeting, check that there is enough light on the platform for you to read your notes.

147

3. Check with the chairman on how long you are to speak. You were told that before you planned your speech, but there may be a last minute change in the program. Check, also, the precise arrangements for questions, discussion, intermission, refreshments, or anything else on the program. You look foolish if you end your speech with a ringing call for questions, and then the chairman jumps up and says, "Before we get around to the questions, I have a few announcements to make, and we shall also have coffee, which I notice is ready now."

So ask, and be sure!

4. If you are to use a blackboard, check that chalk and eraser are at hand. If you have maps, charts, slides, filmstrips or other visual aids, examine them to be sure they are in order. If anyone is to help you (e.g., by operating a projector) be clear about the signals you will give. Politely, yet insistently, get whatever co-operation you need to have materials and equipment in perfect order before the meeting begins. It is better to seem a little fussy behind the scenes that to seem disorganized and incompetent on the platform.

5. If, when you get on the platform, you see that the audience is scattered thinly about the hall, and if the chairman does not move them to the front, do it yourself. An effective way to do this is described in Chapter 20.

Physical Condition

Don't eat heavily just before you speak. It is best to eat two or three hours in advance. When the stomach is loaded with food, it attracts to itself a copious supply of blood. Some of that blood is drawn from the brain, so your thinking is slowed; you may even feel drowsy.

Try to be well rested before you speak. If you have to travel to the meeting, start early so that you can relax before you mount the platform.

Listeners seldom realize how hard a good speaker is working. He seems to be standing at ease, with words flowing effortlessly from his lips. In fact, effective speaking involves a lavish outpouring of energy. So be sure you have the energy to give.

Dress

A general rule that will tell you what to wear on the platform is, "Let your attire be appropriate to the place and to the occasion." If you are in doubt as to what is appropriate, ask and be sure.

Here are some hints concerning details of dress:

1. Don't wear glittering objects. For women, that means bright earrings, necklaces, pins and bracelets. Men should not wear bright lapel badges or gleaming pen-clips in their breast pockets. The danger with such objects is that they reflect light. The crystal, or the metal bracelet of a wrist watch, for example, can flash dazzling beams of light into the auditorium every time you move your arm.

The gaze of a spectator tends to be attracted to the brightest object in his field of vision. Ideally the speaker's face should be the brightest object on the platform. This may not always be so. You cannot exert much control over the lighting equipment of the hall, but you can avoid making your task harder. Don't bring with you bright objects that will keep drawing the gaze of the audience away from your face.

Women can wear jewelry that is beautiful without being highly reflective. If you wear a wristwatch it can have a leather strap, and the face can be turned to the inside of your wrist.

2. For men, dark clothing is best. Dark clothes make the face seem brighter by contrast. Women may not always want to wear dark clothes, but they should at least avoid brilliant colors and bold patterns. A woman should not wear a broad-brimmed hat that would shade her face.

3. Don't let yourself play with parts of your clothing or jewelry. I once saw a woman speaker sliding her wedding ring off and on to her finger. Before long, half the audience was counting the number of times that ring came off, instead of paying attention to the speech.

Spectacles

Do you normally wear spectacles? Then, if you can possibly do without them, remove them for speaking. The lenses prevent spectators from seeing your eyes—and the eyes are an important means of giving expression and emphasis. Worse, the lenses may flash reflections into the eyes of the spectators.

If you are near-sighted, take the spectacles off altogether, read your notes with the naked eye, and put up with not seeing the audience as clearly as you would wish to. You can use the spectacles during question time, while you look at a questioner.

Some far-sighted speakers hold the spectacles in one hand, and raise them to the eyes now and then for a glance at their notes. If this is done boldly and not too often, it is acceptable. It may mean you must train yourself to use the minimum number of notes, but the effort will be well repaid.

Good eye contact between speaker and audience is a powerful aid to communication.

Watches

I have already suggested that a wristwatch should be worn inside the wrist to avoid reflections from the crystal. There is another reason: with the watch in this position, you can keep an eye on the passage of time without letting the audience see what you are doing. This is important. You should be aware of time, but the audience should forget it. If you use a wristwatch, don't let the audience see you consult it; if you have a pocket watch, don't keep hauling it out to look at the time. The best method is to lay your watch on table or lectern where you can see it without seeming to look at it.

Deportment

Most people realize that the speaker's deportment is an indication of his thinking. Here are some hints for producing a favorable impression on the audience.

1. Walk onto the platform briskly. When you sit, hold your body erect.

2. Always stand to speak, even in a small room. When you are standing, your voice is stronger, and the people in the back rows can see you better; and you are in a more powerful position relative to the seated audience.

3. Don't sway from side to side, or to and fro as you speak. Such a motion is distracting to the audience.

Don't stand with one shoulder lower than the other. Some speakers, holding their notes in the right hand, will droop the right shoulder, and vice versa. Watch for this, or get a friend to watch you. Check the habit before it gets established.

4. Don't straddle the feet wide apart. If you are behind a table or lectern, place the feet six to twelve inches apart.

On an open platform, with nothing between you and the audience, you can use your feet to good advantage. The basic position is with feet turned out slightly, and the heel of one foot in line with the other instep and about six inches from it. For relaxation, you can reverse the position of the feet.

In this position, you can shift your weight for expression. In a passive, quiet mood, place your weight on the rear foot; in an active, intense mood, place your weight on the forward foot.

For still greater effect, step forward when you want to add force to a sentence; step backward when you want to moderate the effect of a sentence.

Practice this position before a full-length mirror. See and feel the stance that looks effective and is comfortable for you.

5. If you are not hemmed in by other people on the platform, and if you are not using a microphone, you can move a few paces to one side or the other. The move gives all listeners a slightly different view of you, and tends to heighten their interest.

But don't run out of ideas at the extremity of such a movement, or you will have to rush back to your notes to see what to say next.

And don't let yourself pace rhythmically from side to side like a tiger in a cage. People will stop listening and start counting the number of times you cross the platform.

6. Watch yourself—and get a friend to watch you—for nervous tics and distracting movements.

Men, don't rattle the money in your trousers pocket!

I saw one speaker holding his notes firmly with his left hand and sliding his right thumb and forefinger rhythmically up and down the margin of the sheet. Within minutes, every eye in the audience was on that moving hand.

Drumming with the fingers on table or lectern, tapping the toe of one shoe on the floor, absent-minded winding and rewinding of a watch—don't let such tricks grow into habits.

Remember that, in most cases, your hold on the audience's attention is tenuous. Never do anything that would weaken or break that hold.

Other Platform Activities

If you are to use charts, diagrams or exhibits of any kind, keep them out of sight, or at least covered, until you need them. If they are in sight from the beginning, people will keep looking at them and wondering about them.

In turning over charts, displaying exhibits, etc. try not to turn your back on the audience. Don't even divert your gaze from them for long.

For example, you uncover a diagram and, facing the audience, say, "This is a cross section of the Great Pyramid of Gizeh, and here is the King's Chamber."

On the word "here," you glance at the chart so as to put your pointer in the right place. But you at once face the audience again, and keep facing them until the next time you have to glance at the diagram.

When you look, for any appreciable time, away from the audience, you have lost control of them. Moreover, as your eyes turn away, your head tends to turn, too, and your voice does not carry properly into the auditorium.

Don't pass anything around the audience during a speech! Exhibits, photographs, printed matter—no matter what it is—will distract the audience's attention from you. Have such things handed out or inspected after you have finished speaking.

Undesirable Antics

I have heard of speakers taking their jackets off "to attract the attention of the audience," removing their ties part way through "to revive interest" and firing off blank-cartridge pistols "to wake up the audience." Such antics are confessions that the speaker is incompetent.

If you have planned your opening properly, what you say will attract the attention of the audience.

If you have constructed the body of your speech properly, you will hold the interest of the audience by awakening and sustaining a lively sense of personal concern with your subject. (If the subject does not concern any member of the audience, you should not be using that subject, anyway.)

If your delivery is animated and varied, nobody will fall asleep, so there will be no need of explosions to awaken them.

If you want to be a clown, be a clown by all means, but join a circus! If you want to be a speaker, be a good speaker. The accepted techniques of speaking are sufficient to capture, and hold, and move the feelings of, any audience.

Summary

Prepare for the meeting by:
1. Typing a sheet of personal information.
2. Checking platform and lighting.
3. Checking timing and order of program.
4. Checking materials and equipment.
5. Getting the audience together.

Get yourself in good physical condition to speak.

Dress appropriately:
1. Don't wear glittering objects.
2. Don't wear brilliant colors or bold patterns.
3. Don't play with clothing or jewelry.

If you can, dispense with spectacles.

Keep aware of the time; let the audience forget it.

Good deportment creates a favorable impression.

Don't let exhibits distract attention from your speech.

A good speaker need not be a clown.

15. Introducing a Speaker

Who, or why, or which, or what,
Is the Akond of Swat?

EDWARD LEAR

Usually each important speaker at a meeting is introduced to the audience. Sometimes the chairman makes the introduction; sometimes other people do it. Properly delivered, the introduction aids the speaker, and contributes much to the success of the meeting. The following hints will help you deliver an effective introduction.

Functions of the Introduction

1. The introduction helps to settle the audience after the stir of arrival, after a meal or an intermission, or after the applause that followed a previous speech.

2. The thoughts of the audience are diffused, each person's mind on a different track. The introduction unifies the thinking of the audience and directs their attention toward the subject of the forthcoming speech.

3. The introduction establishes the authority of the speaker; it tells why, on this subject, he is worth listening to. It tells the audience things about the speaker that conventional modesty prevents his saying about himself.

4. The introduction begins to establish the correct tone. Remember, the audience will have an emotional, as well as an intellectual experience. So set the right emotional tone. If the subject is light,

154

use a light tone; if it is serious, don't crack jokes in the introduction.

5. The introduction gives the speaker time to collect his thoughts. He may have been caught up in the pre-meeting bustle; he may have been chatting over dinner, or listening to the previous speaker. Now, during the introduction, he can concentrate on what he is going to say.

Preparing the Introduction

Your material should be accurate. Check it with the speaker if you can. Be sure that you have these points correct.

1. Surname, first name and initials. Check with him about the pronunciation of his name if you have the slightest doubt about it.

2. His rank, title or degrees, if any.

3. His occupation.

4. Any official positions that he holds, e.g., mayor of such-and-such a city; president of this or that society.

5. Any special knowledge or experience concerning the subject.

6. Any other relevant qualifications, e.g., being the author of a book on the subject.

7. *Exact* subject of speech.

Much of this material can be found out in advance, from the organizers of the meeting or, with prominent persons, from *Who's Who* reference books, and business or professional directories.

But it is a good idea to ask the speaker if there is anything particular he would like you to mention. He might say, "Yes, you can mention that today I received word that the ABC Foundation is giving me a grant for research into the street numbering system of ancient Babylon."

Also ask him if there is anything he does not want you to mention. He might say, "I'm rather tired of hearing about that amateur boxing championship I won in college. It's not really relevant to my work nowadays." Or he might say, "I'd rather you didn't mention my book *Shakespeare Was a Woman*. I've recently revised my thinking on that subject."

Make notes of all the information you gather, by research, or from the speaker.

Delivering the Introduction

1. Begin with a sentence that clearly indicates what you are talking about.

Ladies and gentlemen, it is my pleasant duty to introduce to you the main speaker of the evening, Mr. So-and-So. . . .

2. Mention the subject. Say, *briefly,* that it is interesting and important to this audience.

Mr. So-and-So is going to speak on "Traffic Problems, Their Causes and Solution." I know the difficulty that many of you have to get to and from work each day. I know the difficulty most of you had to get here this evening. I'll confidently say that this subject is a most interesting one to all of us.

This is enough to say concerning the subject—about fifty words. *Don't* plunge into a long discussion of the subject, or you will be stealing the speaker's thunder.

3. The main part of your introduction is your description of the speaker and his qualifications. Here you bring out the information you obtained in advance.

Mention the speaker's name at least three times. Some introducers don't do this; they hold the name back, mentioning it only once at the end. That is not a good practice. The audience soon notices that you are dodging the speaker's name and are using various substitutes—"this outstanding citizen . . . this distinguished man . . . our speaker . . . this highly qualified expert" and so on. Moreover, there may be some in the audience who do not know the speaker's name, so mention it several times to be sure they get it.

4. Last comes the formal call upon the speaker. There is one conventional phrase for this—"And now it gives me great pleasure to call upon Mr. So-and-So."

This formal call *must be given.* Every experienced speaker expects it. If, as is probable, he is not paying much attention to you, but is thinking over his opening, the formal call serves as a trigger to snap him out of his thoughtful mood and prepare him to speak.

If you end in some unconventional way, the speaker may not realize you are finished. So use the accepted formula and be safe.

As you deliver the formal call, you can turn and look at the speaker; if you wish, you can give a slight bow or a gesture toward him.

There should be some applause at this point, during which you sit down, and the speaker moves to the lectern or microphone.

5. An introduction should last not more than five minutes! Long introductions are boring to the audience and nerve-racking for the main speaker.

A Sample Introduction

Ladies and Gentlemen, it is my pleasant duty to introduce to you the main speaker of the evening, Doctor Virgil Brahms, who will speak to us on the subject, "The Artist and the Computer." This subject forms a fitting and fascinating conclusion to our series of lectures on "Art Through the Ages."

Doctor Brahms is exceptionally well qualified to speak about "The Artist and the Computer." He is a well-known poet. He tells me he published his first poem, in a children's magazine, when he was seven years old. He has continued to write and publish poetry ever since. His latest book, *Collected Poems of a Music-Lover,* was published last Christmas by Gutenberg and Caxton.

Doctor Brahms is even better known as a musician. He is Professor of Music at Christopher Columbus Memorial University. To name only two of his recent major works: he composed the music for last season's Off-Broadway hit show, "Not a Sound Was Heard," and his "Mass for Atheists" was released last month by Groovy Disks Incorporated.

In the last three years, Doctor Brahms has devoted much of his time to studying the application of the computer to the arts of the poet and the composer. He has had a powerful computer installed in his department at Christopher Columbus; with it, he and his graduate students have conducted an extensive research program.

In Doctor Brahms's new opera, "Death of a Programmer" the words, music and strobe light effects have been composed and arranged entirely by the computer. "Death of a Programmer" receives its world premiere in New York, in three months' time.

You'll agree, I'm sure, that we couldn't have found a more authoritative speaker on the subject, "The Artist and the Computer."

And now it gives me great pleasure to call upon Doctor Virgil Brahms.

What Not to Do

1. Don't begin with, "This speaker needs no introduction." It is absurd to say this, and then go on and deliver the introduction. However well known the speaker may be, there will be some people present who don't know all about him. So make the introduction and omit the apologies.

2. Don't include the phrase, "You didn't come here to listen to me." It's true; but why belittle yourself and the introduction? The audience will gladly listen to you, if you are *brief*.

3. Don't overpraise the speaker. Describe his abilities and accomplishments in favorable terms, but don't make it sound as if he is Demosthenes and Leonardo da Vinci and Abraham Lincoln all rolled into one. Excessive praise embarrasses the speaker and makes the audience sceptical.

4. Don't talk about yourself. You may be tempted to do this if you have some knowledge of the subject. Resist the temptation!

5. Don't tell jokes. You often hear them in introductions, but they are usually unwelcome. A humorous story concerning the speaker is permissible, *if* it is in good taste, *if* it will produce a favorable reaction from the audience toward the speaker (i.e., if it will increase their interest in him, or their respect for him) and *if* it is appropriate to the tone of the coming speech.

6. Don't try to make an introduction without notes. You risk the horrible fiasco of saying, "And now, it gives me great pleasure to call upon . . . er . . . to call upon. . . ." You have forgotten the speaker's name.

7. Don't rush, and don't fade out, on the formal call. Deliver it slowly and loudly.

Summary

Functions of the introduction are:
    1. Settle the audience.

2. Unify the thoughts of the audience.
3. Establish the authority of the speaker.
4. Set the correct tone.
5. Let the speaker collect his thoughts.

Check the details mentioned in an introduction.

Form of the introduction:

1. Indicate briefly what you are about to say.
2. Touch briefly on the subject.
3. Describe the speaker and his qualifications.
4. Formally call upon the speaker to speak.
5. Maximum length, five minutes.

Don't over-praise the speaker.

Don't say too much about the subject.

Don't talk about yourself.

Don't tell jokes.

Don't omit the formal call.

Exercise

Choose some famous person, real or fictional, living or dead. Prepare and deliver an introduction to a speech by him on an appropriate subject. Here are a few examples:

George Washington on ''The theory and practice of revolution.''

Cleopatra on ''Julius Caesar.''

Jesse James on ''Crime does not pay.''

Romeo Montague on ''Teen-age marriage.''

Louisa May Alcott on ''Writing for children.''

Socrates on ''The art of conversation.''

Orville Wright on ''The future of the flying machine.''

Othello on ''Race prejudice.''

Mark Twain on ''Life on the Mississippi.''

Benjamin Franklin on ''Hard work, the key to success.''

Christopher Columbus on ''The new route to the Indies.''

Emily Dickinson on ''The pleasures of solitude''

16. Various Short Speech Forms

Brief words, when actions wait, are well.
FRANCIS BRETT HARTE

You will sometimes have to make short speeches for a variety of purposes—welcoming a guest, presenting a gift, proposing a toast, and so on. The following suggestions will help you plan and deliver such speeches easily and effectively.

Toasts

A toast is a public demonstration of affection or respect for a person or institution. A three-point formula will serve for all toasts.

1. *Opening.* Explain what you are talking about. "Ladies and Gentlemen, it is my pleasant duty to propose the toast to . . ."

2. *Body.* Recount, briefly, forcefully and pleasantly, why the person or institution deserves esteem. This is no time for a balanced character analysis of a person or a critical survey of an institution. Mention only pleasant and positive items. Remember that many members of your audience already know the facts, so be brief and tactful in reviewing them. A personal note is usually welcome in a toast: "Why *I* admire So-and-so . . ." This makes your speech different from any others on the same subject.

Be brief. Nobody wants to hear long speeches at such a time. Don't strain excessively for humor, particularly if you are not used to telling jokes in public. Certainly don't tell off-color jokes;

they will offend at least some of the guests. Don't tell embarrassing anecdotes about people who are present; your duty is to give pleasure, not pain. Be sincere! If you cannot honestly say something pleasant, don't accept the responsibility of proposing the toast.

3. *Formal call.* "Ladies and Gentlemen, I call on you to rise and drink to the health of So-and-so."

You may have to reply to a toast. All that is required here is a few words of thanks for the kindness, good wishes, etc. that have been expressed. Prepare a few such remarks for your reply, but also, if you can, add a reference to something that was said in an earlier speech.

Banquet Speeches

It is hard to speak at banquets. If you speak before the meal, your audience is eager to get at the food, and begrudges the time spent in listening to you. If you speak after the meal, people are partly stupefied with food and drink; some of them want to go to the washroom; others want to go home.

Don't undertake banquet speeches until you have had some experience in easier conditions.

When you do speak at a banquet, these tips will help:

1. Make a particularly strong appeal to the interest of the audience. Stimulate a sense of personal concern; explain why the subject is important to them.

2. Be bright. A lively, cheerful tone is appropriate.

3. Be forceful. Use no "ifs," "buts" or "maybes." Drive each point home, hard.

4. Make yourself heard. Many banquet rooms are acoustically dead. Use much more power than you would for the same audience in an auditorium. Articulate perfectly.

5. Keep your watch in front of you, and be brief. Ask the chairman what your time limit is. If he says, "Fifteen minutes," speak for twelve. If he says, "Thirty minutes," speak for twenty-five.

6. If you are to speak after the meal, eat little or nothing so that you, at least, are not stupefied. A full stomach draws blood from the brain and slows your thinking.

Welcoming a Visitor

The structure of a speech of welcome is much like that of an introduction.

1. Explain what you are talking about. "On behalf of the Ourtown Civic Betterment Association, it is my pleasure to welcome Mr. So-and-so."

2. Tell the audience something about the visitor. As in an introduction, be pleasant and positive. Mention the good points and avoid criticisms. Mention the purpose of his visit. (Don't assume that every listener already knows this.)

3. End with a formal phrase of welcome. "So, Mr. So-and-so, it gives me great pleasure to welcome you to Ourtown."

Here, as in preparing an introduction, it will be helpful to talk with the visitor and find out if there is anything he wants you to say, or not to say.

Presenting a Gift

1. Tell them what you are going to tell them. "Ladies and Gentlemen, I have been appointed by the Ourtown Civic Betterment Association to make a presentation to our retiring President, Mr. John Goodfellow."

2. Explain the reason for the gift, e.g., "Twenty years' devoted service." Say something pleasant about the recipient. A personal touch is appropriate—your own recollections or impressions of the recipient. If necessary, say something about the gift itself—why the particular article was chosen. Or, if the gift is an intangible object—for example, a scholarship—you may have to describe or explain it.

3. Make the formal presentation. "And now, Mr. Goodfellow, it gives me great pleasure to present you with this set of luggage, and one-way ticket to Timbuctoo."

Accepting a Gift

1. Make a preliminary expression of thanks, e.g., "Friends, I am deeply grateful to the Ourtown Civic Betterment Association for this delightful gift."

2. Comment, from your point of view, on the donor-recipient relationship. Speak personally and pleasantly of your dealings with the organization that has made the gift. If necessary, comment on the gift itself.

3. End with a formal sentence of acceptance, and with some pleasant remark about the future. ''My thanks go to the executive and members for this thoughtful, useful gift. I can assure you that this pleasant occasion marks only the end of my official duties. It does not alter my interest in the Association, or my devotion to its work.''

If you knew the gift was coming, don't pretend in your speech that it was unexpected. Simplicity, sincerity and brevity are the key principles for acceptance speeches.

Thanking a Speaker

1. *Opening.* Indicate your aim. ''Mr. Chairman, Ladies and Gentlemen, I want to thank Mr. So-and-so for his interesting speech.''

2. *Body.* Say *a few* sentences about the speech itself. For this purpose, it will be useful to take brief notes while the speech is going on, picking out a point that you think will suit your purpose. Mention that point, indicating why it was particularly interesting or helpful to the audience, or to you personally. Or mention briefly that the theme was helpful and interesting.

3. *Formal expression of thanks.* ''Mr. So-and-so, on behalf of the Ourtown Civic Betterment Association, I thank you for coming here tonight, and for giving us, so entertainingly, the benefit of your experience and your thinking on this important subject.''

For thanking a speaker, take two minutes at the outside, preferably less. It is a pleasant formality, but remember that people don't want to listen to you at this time. They are interested in getting on to the next speaker, or in going home.

Making an Announcement

An announcement should be accurate and complete. Make sure you have *correct* information and *all* the information. It is humiliating, after you have made a lengthy announcement, to hear some-one shout, ''Where is it being held?'' or ''What time is it?'' or to have the chairman say, ''I'm afraid I shall have to make a correction to that announcement.''

Here is a list of points to get *in writing* for an effective announcement.

1. The nature of the activity, with a detailed description including, if necessary, a statement of its purpose (e.g., ''to raise money for the club's building fund.'')

2. Date.

3. Time.

4. Place. Transportation information, if needed.

5. Admission fee. Conditions of admission, if there are any. (e.g., members only; or each member is entitled to bring one guest.)

6. Where to get tickets.

7. A specific appeal to attend, if needed. This may have to be a short persuasive speech, employing emotional appeals to the listeners, playing on their curiosity, loyalty, etc.

After giving all the details and making any necessary appeal for support, end by repeating the nature of the event, the place, time and date.

Use your notes for announcements, and reduce the risk of making mistakes.

Summary

Formula for toasts:

    1. Explain your purpose.

    2. Recount the grounds for esteem.

    3. The formal call.

Banquet speeches are difficult:

    1. Be sure to stimulate personal concern.

    2. Be bright.

    3. Be forceful.

    4. Make yourself heard.

    5. Be brief.

    6. Don't eat too much.

Speeches of welcome:

    1. Explain your purpose.

2. Describe the visitor; explain his visit.

3. Formal phrase of welcome.

Presenting a gift:

1. Explain your purpose.

2. Explain the reason for the gift.

3. Formal presentation.

Accepting a gift:

1. Preliminary expression of thanks.

2. Discuss donor-recipient relationship.

3. Formal acceptance.

Thanking a speaker:

1. Explain your purpose.

2. Comment briefly on the speech.

3. Formal expression of thanks.

Making an announcement:

1. Get relevant information in writing.

2. Be sure you give all the facts.

3. Make an appeal for action, if needed.

4. End by repeating the key facts.

Exercises

1. Prepare a toast to some person or organization of your choice.

2. Make a gift-presentation speech to some person of your choice, selecting an appropriate imaginary gift.

3. Prepare an announcement for some activity—concert, dance, bingo, clambake, etc.—in aid of some cause of your choice. Include a strong appeal for support.

17. Impromptu Speaking

*The necessity of being ready increases—Look
to it.*

ABRAHAM LINCOLN

When you become known as a speaker, you will find that, from
time to time, you are called on to speak impromptu. Strictly defined, impromptu or extemporaneous speaking means *speaking
without notice and without preparation.* It is difficult, and requires
considerable experience and self-confidence.

But there should never be any need for pure impromptu speaking. If you are alert, you will not be caught completely unprepared.
So in this chapter we shall discuss means of speaking effectively
on short notice and with little preparation.

Be Prepared

Suppose you are at a public meeting where speeches are to be
made, and you are not one of the announced speakers. You can
easily assess the chances of your being called on to speak.

If you are an anonymous unit in a large audience, you certainly
will not be asked to speak.

If you are at the head table of the banquet, or on the platform
of the meeting, or if you are a prominent member of the organization, your situation is different. Let us analyze the possibilities.

1. If all scheduled speakers turn up, and the program is long
enough to fill the time available, you will not be called.

2. If one of the speakers fails to turn up, or takes much less
than his allotted time, and if the program seems likely to fall short

of the expected duration, then the chairman may ask someone else to speak. That someone may be you, particularly if you are known to be a competent speaker.

3. If the chairman has already started calling on unscheduled speakers, and if he is looking around for more, and his gaze falls on you, then he is likely to call you.

If, in any circumstances, you have the slightest suspicion that you may be called to speak, begin to prepare. *Never let yourself be caught unprepared.*

If you are called, the audience will not know you have been preparing; they will be impressed to hear you deliver a coherent, well-rounded speech, apparently without a moment's thought.

Here is an example from my own experience. I was at a Boy Scouts' concert, simply one of several hundred people in a large auditorium. There seemed not the slightest chance that I would have to speak. But things kept going wrong backstage; there was delay after delay. The Master of Ceremonies had to struggle, again and again, to fill in time. This was still none of my business, and normally there would have been no risk of my being asked to speak. But in this instance, the Master of Ceremonies was a former student of my public speaking course, and he knew I was in the audience!

I jotted down a few notes and was prepared to make a short, amusing speech about scouting.

I did not have to deliver it; the backstage hitches were straightened out and the concert rolled on smoothly. But the M.C. admitted afterward that he was just on the point of calling me.

It is better to prepare a speech and not deliver it than to be forced to speak unprepared.

Qualities of the Impromptu Speech

1. The subject is usually chosen for you by the nature of the meeting. At the Scout concert, it would have been absurd for me to speak on "The Gold Standard" or "Subsidy Of The Arts." I had to plan a speech on scouting. But at a banquet organized by an authors' association, I would obviously have to say something about writers and writing.

2. Although the audience thinks it is unplanned, the impromptu

speech should have the proper speech structure: opening, body, and conclusion.

3. The impromptu speech is short. No one expects you to produce a well-researched, thirty-minute speech at the drop of a hat. For impromptu work, set your sights at three to five minutes.

4. Therefore it is sufficient to make one or two points in the body of the speech.

Planning the Impromptu Speech

1. Define your theme. Usually, as we have seen, you have little choice of subject. But you must think what you will say about the subject, what main impression you wish to leave with the audience when your speech is done. In Chapter 3, theme definition was discussed with reference to prepared speeches; a good theme is no less important for the impromptu speech.

Without it, you will not have a real speech, only "a few remarks."

2. Analyze your audience. You are going to *communicate* with them; so what do you know about them?

a) What do they know about the subject?

b) What do they *feel* about the subject? What are their beliefs, hopes, fears and prejudices about it?

c) What have they heard about the subject already at the meeting?

d) Are most of them favorably or unfavorably inclined toward my theme?

e) What is their mood—serious or light-hearted?

3. Choose your opening. For impromptu speaking the *timely reference* is usually easy and appropriate. Refer to something that has been said or done at the meeting; refer to the purpose of the meeting, or to some current concern of the organization that arranged the meeting.

The *personal reference* is also suitable and easy. You must have some interest in, or connection with, the subject, or you would not be at the meeting.

Deliver the opening sentence, then proceed at once to tell them what you are going to tell them. State your theme and arouse their interest by saying briefly why the theme is important to them.

4. Arrange the body of the speech. Select one or two points

that will support your theme. Decide what means you will use to demonstrate those points. Remember the three-fold process for making each point—state, demonstrate, recapitulate.

For one of your points, it is often appropriate to take something that has been said by an earlier speaker, but not fully developed by him.

You can endorse the other speaker's view, supporting it with extra arguments, evidence, illustrations or emotional appeals, or you can refute the other speaker's view.

But don't spend all your time on other speakers' material; make, if you can, one new point.

5. Plan your conclusion. One concluding technique will suffice for all impromptu work; restate the theme. For variety, let the restatement be worded differently—more forcibly—than the opening statement of the theme. If it is appropriate, follow the restatement of the theme with a call for action.

No Apologies

Don't apologize, after or before an impromptu speech, for the fact that it is short. Don't complain that you had no time to prepare. Simply stand up, make the speech, take the applause, and sit down.

Summary

Don't be caught unprepared.
When speaking impromptu:
    1. Take an appropriate subject.
    2. Use proper structure—opening, body, conclusion.
    3. Be brief.
    4. Make only one or two points.
To plan the impromptu speech:
    1. Define your theme.
    2. Analyze your audience.
    3. Use timely reference or personal reference opening.
    4. In the body, refer to what has been said or done.
    5. For a conclusion, restate the theme.
Don't apologize for your speech.

Exercise

Open a book at random and stick a pin into a page. Speak for two minutes on the word the pin has pierced, or on the nearest meaningful word. (Obviously, you won't speak on "the," "but," or "and," but nearly all verbs and nouns can serve as subjects.)

18. Debates and Panel Discussions

Great argument about it and about . . .
OMAR KHAYYAM

A debate is a small-scale reproduction of the proceedings of a legislature. There are two kinds of debate, *theoretical* and *practical*.

1. *The theoretical debate* is conducted to air the views of the participants, and to give them an enjoyable exercise in public speaking. It often deals with subjects of wide interest and great importance, approving or condemning something that is going on in the world, or recommending a solution to a contemporary problem. Theoretical debates might revolve around the following subjects:

"State lotteries should be used to reduce direct taxes."

"This country should more vigorously support the United Nations."

"Proportional representation should be substituted for the straight majority vote in public elections."

"Trade unions are too powerful for the good of their members."

"Corporal punishment should be more widely used for crimes of violence."

In a theoretical debate, the pros and cons of the subject will be discussed, but *no action will follow*.

2. *The practical debate* is conducted to decide on some course of action. A parent-teacher association, a trade-union local, a city

council, debates a subject within its jurisdiction and decides what to do about it.

"This association shall hold a dance to raise money for the scholarship fund."

"This local shall levy a special assessment to pay convention expenses for delegates and observers."

"This council shall call tenders for construction of a new art gallery-museum complex."

The pros and cons of the subject are debated, the motion is passed or defeated, and something does or does not happen as a result.

Theoretical Debates

A chairman supervises the debates, and there are four principal speakers.

1. Speaker A proposes the motion in a prepared speech, usually of about twenty minutes. He ends formally, "Therefore, Mr. Chairman, I propose that. . . . (enunciating the motion)"

2. Speaker B opposes the motion in a prepared speech of the same length, ending, "Therefore, Mr. Chairman, I oppose the motion."

3. Speaker C seconds the motion in a speech of about ten minutes, ending, "Therefore, Mr. Chairman, I second the motion."

4. Speaker D seconds the opposition in a speech of about ten minutes, ending, "Therefore, Mr. Chairman, I second the opposition to this motion."

(Speeches 3 and 4 will be partly prepared in advance, partly devoted to refuting the arguments put forward by Speakers B and A, respectively.)

5. Next there are speeches from the floor, usually with a short time limit. If you intend to speak in a debate, prepare a few ideas in advance, also support or oppose something said by an earlier speaker. This is good practice in impromptu speaking.

6. Speaker B sums up the case for the opposition.

7. Speaker A sums up the case for the motion.

8. The chairman calls for a vote on the motion and announces the result.

Practical Debates

The practical debate takes place during the business meeting of some organization and is conducted less formally than the theoretical debate.

Usually a member proposes a motion and says what he has to say in favor of it. Another member says, "I second the motion" and may or may not make a speech.

The President then calls for discussion of the motion; members express their opinions for or against it. Here is the basic plan for a speech in these circumstances.

1. *Opening.* State your position. "Mr. President, I want to support the motion," or "Mr. President, I oppose this motion."

2. *Body.* Endorse or refute points made by other speakers, and state any points that have not been mentioned.

3. *Conclude with a clear call for action.* "So, Mr. President, I call on all members to vote in favor of this motion," or "So, Mr. President, this proposal is highly dangerous to the future of our organization. Let us reject the motion once and for all."

Debating Strategy

Some contingencies may call for a little strategy in planning and delivering your speech.

Suppose you are strongly opposed to the motion, yet you can tell, from your knowledge of the membership, and from the tone of the discussion, that it is certain to pass. You have three possible courses of action:

1. You know you cannot change the course of events, and you feel you can do more good in the future if you don't irritate the executive and the majority of the membership now. So you keep quiet.

2. In the same situation, you make a short speech, mildly opposing the motion—taking the "soft line."

3. But suppose you do not mind irritating the executive and majority, and you feel, for your conscience's sake, that you must put your opinions on record. Then you take the "hard line." "Mr. President, this is one of the most outrageous, undemocratic, un-

constitutional proposals that I've ever heard in my fifteen years' membership of this organization, etc.''

Suppose you are opposed to the motion, and from the tone of the discussion you know it is likely to pass; yet from your knowledge of the membership, you think there is a chance of swinging enough votes to reject the motion. It would be indiscreet to take the hard line. By harshly attacking the majority, you would alienate them and ruin your chance of winning their votes. This is indubitably the time to take the soft line, and to deliver a tactful, persuasive speech.

''Mr. President, this is a most interesting motion and, as Mr. P and Miss Q have so ably pointed out, it does have several attractive features. I agree that it would do this, that and the other. I agree that, on the surface, this would seem to benefit the organization. But. . . .'' and you lead tactfully into your arguments against the motion.

''If you will persuade, you must first please,'' said Lord Chesterfield. You please your listeners by seeming to agree with them. Begin at a point of agreement and lead, by degrees, toward the points on which you disagree. Study Mark Antony's speech, analyzed in Chapter 6, as an example of the soft-line approach to an audience that at first was hostile.

Suppose that, as sometimes happens, the executive tries to rush a motion through without any discussion. The usual technique is that a member proposes the motion as briefly as he can. Another member quietly seconds it. The President immediately calls for a vote.

MEMBER X: Mr. President, I propose that the annual dues of this Association be doubled.

MEMBER Y: I second that.

PRESIDENT: All those in favor. . . .

Slipped in among a series of routine motions, this sort of thing can pass before most members realize what they are voting on.

To oppose it, you must act fast. Jump up before the President can put it to the vote and say, ''Mr. President, before you call for the vote, I would like to speak to that motion.''

If there is any pretense of democracy in the organization, he will have to let you speak. But the motion was a surprise to you; you have no speech prepared. How can you oppose it effectively?

Stall for time. In the emergency, let yourself ramble for a minute or two. Make a few vague remarks that call for little thought on your part. While you are rambling like this, three-quarters of your brain is clicking away, marshalling the arguments you will use in the body of your speech. Here is how such an opening might go.

Mr. President, I was rather surprised—I might even say I was shocked—when I heard the wording of that motion. If my hearing serves me right, it was that the annual dues of this Association be doubled. If the wording is not exactly right, that, at least, was the sense of the motion.

Now it's true that costs are going up all around us. It only takes a comparison of the current grocery bill with one for twelve months, or even six months ago, to illustrate that point.

But doesn't this seem a rather large increase, doubling the dues?

Why, I've been a member of this Association for eight years, and I've never heard of such a large increase in one step.

Moreover, Mr. President, I do feel that when such a critical and far-reaching change is in view, we, the members should have had good notice, so that there could be ample consideration and discussion before it was brought to a vote.

This would normally be a weak opening. But it has served its purpose. It has given you time to think, and has given other members time to realize what is going on. Now you are ready to proceed with the body of your speech.

"Now, Mr. President, I suggest there are three reasons why the dues should not be increased at this time . . ."

Train yourself to speak effectively in practical debates. You will find it exciting and gratifying; you will make important contributions to the organizations you belong to, and the society you live in.

Panel Discussions

The panel discussion is superseding the theoretical debate as a means of publicly examining controversial subjects, and as an exercise in public speaking.

In a panel discussion there is no formal taking of sides; there is no motion to be passed or defeated; there may be as many points of view as there are speakers.

A common arrangement is to have a chairman and four speakers. The chairman introduces the speakers all at once, before the discussion begins. Alternatively, he may introduce each speaker just before calling on him to speak.

1. Each speaker delivers a prepared speech, commonly of about 10 minutes.

2. The speakers discuss the subject informally, each commenting on what the others have said, and adding such new ideas as may come to him. This discussion may last twenty minutes.

3. The meeting is thrown open to questions from the floor. A question may be directed to one platform speaker, or to the whole panel. Speeches from the floor are sometimes allowed.

4. Each platform speaker takes a minute or two to sum up his opinions on the subject.

Here are some suggestions that will help panel discussions run smoothly and make them more interesting.

The Platform Speakers

1. Be sure you know how long you are allowed for your opening speech; don't run over the time limit.

2. In preparing your speech, be specific, be personal. Give *your* point of view, *your* experience of the subject.

For example, I heard a panel discussion on ''What do we expect from education?'' All the speakers discussed the subject in an abstract, theoretical way. All had been to school, of course, and all of them, as it happened, were parents of school-age children. They should have mentioned, ''What I feel I missed in school was. . .''; ''Looking back on my school days, the thing I enjoyed most was. . .''; ''My son wants to study so-and-so, but the school only offers. . .''; ''My daughter doesn't seem to be learning to read properly and I think that. . .'' and so on.

Abandon false modesty. Speak personally. It will lead to an interesting, helpful discussion.

3. Some panelists speak sitting down. It is better for you and for the audience if you stand. If preceding speakers have remained seated, stand all the same and say, ''If you don't mind, Mr. Chair-

man, I prefer to speak standing up.'' Several times I have heard this statement draw a round of applause from the audience!

4. In the discussion period, don't slip into holding a quiet conversation with your fellow panelists. Reply by name to the other speaker, but keep your face to the audience and keep projecting. ''I'd like to comment on what Mr. A has just said. It seems to me that. . .''

5. Remember that it is a discussion, not an argument. Keep your temper, even if other speakers criticize you sharply. Let others get angry if they want to; you obtain an advantage by keeping calm.

6. As the discussion proceeds, jot down a few notes for your final summing up. Opinions expressed by other speakers and questions asked by the audience will show you what most needs to be said in conclusion. In your final speech, keep within your time limit.

The Chairman

1. The general principles of chairmanship apply here. But one problem is particularly annoying at panel discussions—when the chairman lets the first three speakers ramble on far beyond their time limits and then has to tell the last speaker, ''I'm sorry, Mr. D, but we can allow you only two minutes, if we are to have any time for discussion and questions.''

Tell the speakers, before you begin, that you are going to hold them to their time limits. Explain *to the audience* as well, that the discussion must run on schedule if everyone is to have his fair chance to speak. Then be ruthless. When a speaker has gone one minute beyond his time limit, stand up and interrupt him. Smile and say, ''Thank you, Mr. A. We shall hear more from you during the discussion period. But now, in fairness to the other members of the panel, I'll have to call on the next speaker.''

2. If one speaker tries to monopolize the discussion period, be firm with him. Shut him up tactfully and, by questions, get the other speakers talking. ''Now, Mr. B, what do you think about such-and-such a point?''

3. You may occasionally find a panel of speakers who are sluggish in discussing the subject. To guard against the meeting falling flat in this way, take notes, while the prepared speeches are being

made, of various points that seem worthy of discussion. Then you can throw these points out to the panel and call for comments on them. This will usually get the discussion moving.

The Audience

Keep pen and paper at hand during the prepared speeches and platform discussion; note the points on which you want to ask questions or make comments later.

Take every opportunity to speak from the floor. Every speech increases your self-confidence and develops your speaking technique.

Summary

Theoretical debate—discussion but no action.
Practical debate—discussion followed by action.
Theoretical debate format:
    1. A proposes the motion.
    2. B opposes the motion.
    3. C seconds the motion.
    4. D seconds the opposition.
    5. Speeches from the floor.
    6. B sums up for the opposition.
    7. A sums up for the motion.
    8. The vote.
Practical debate format:
    1. The motion is proposed.
    2. The motion is seconded.
    3. Discussion.
    4. The vote.
Format for speech in discussion:
    1. State your position.
    2. Endorse or refute other speakers; add new points.
    3. Call for action.
In opposing a motion that is going to pass, you can:
    1. Say nothing.
    2. Take the "soft line."
    3. Take the "hard line."

To sway votes, use your best persuasive technique.

When planning a speech on your feet, stall for time.

Panel discussion format:

    1. Main speakers deliver speeches.

    2. Speakers discuss the subject.

    3. Questions and speeches from the floor.

    4. Main speakers briefly sum up.

Hints for panel speakers:

    1. Keep to your time limit.

    2. Be specific, be personal.

    3. Stand to speak.

    4. During discussion, speak to audience.

    5. Keep your temper.

    6. Take notes for your summing up.

Hints for panel chairman:

    1. Hold speakers to their time limits.

    2. Don't let one speaker monopolize the discussion.

    3. Spark the discussion, if need be, with questions.

Exercises

1. Choose a controversial subject and stage a theoretical debate. You will get best results if there are two well-contrasted sides to the subject.

2. Choose a subject in which there are several possible points of view, and stage a panel discussion.

19. Questions, Opposition and Distractions

Anyone can hold the helm when the sea is calm.
PUBLILIUS SYRUS

In this chapter we shall examine several problems that the speaker may encounter, and suggest ways to solve them.

Questions

Some beginning speakers dread being asked questions. This fear can be overcome by accustoming yourself to answering questions in practice sessions. A helpful thought is this: you have prepared yourself on the subject of your speech, so you probably know more about it than most of the audience.

When you agree to speak at any function, find out if you will be expected to answer questions and, if so, what portion of the meeting will be devoted to questions. The presence of a question period may affect your planning. For example, there may be some point concerning the subject which, you think, might not be of much interest to the audience. Instead of developing that point fully, you can mention it briefly and suggest that anyone who is interested should ask a question about it.

As for the Alberta tar-sands, and the methods of extracting oil from them, I'm not going into any detail. If anyone would like to hear more about those deposits, please ask about them during the question period.

It is good strategy to leave several potentially interesting items dangling in mid-air like this. You improve the prospects of a lively and instructive question period.

Question Procedure

There are three common procedures for putting questions.

1. A member of the audience addresses his question straight to the speaker. This method is used in small, informal meetings.

Your answer will mean little to the audience unless they know what the question was, so, if the questioner did not speak loudly and clearly, repeat the question. (This repetition gives you time to think of your answer.)

2. Questions are addressed to the chairman. This more formal procedure is common in large meetings. If there is need for repetion of the question, the chairman repeats it, then the speaker replies. This method, also, gives the speaker time to think of his reply. It reduces the risk of questioners' getting into arguments with the speaker.

3. Questions are written and passed to the chairman, who reads them aloud. This method is best for the speaker. The questions are shorter and more comprehensible than spoken ones. There is even less risk than with method 2 of audience-speaker arguments.

Answering Questions

1. While listening to a spoken question, look steadily at the questioner. This shows him you are attentive, and helps you to understand what he is saying.

2. In replying to spoken questions, some beginning speakers drop to a conversational voice, just because they feel they are speaking to one person. Don't do this, but answer questions in your full speaking voice, so everyone can hear.

3. Don't begin your reply with "That's a good question," or "I'm glad you asked that question." These phrases have been worn out by excessive use.

4. If you cannot understand the question, ask the questioner

to define some term he has used. This will usually clarify what he is driving at.

For example, after you have spoken on crime prevention, a questioner asks:

Now, Mr. Speaker, what do you think of these so-called new methods that we read about so much in the papers, and hear discussed on radio and TV nowadays? Are they really any improvement on the tried and tested methods?

How can you reply? Does he mean electronic eavesdropping and communication devices? Does he mean changes in police organization, prison administration, courtroom, parole or probation procedures?

Ask him:

Exactly what methods are you referring to, sir?

He replies:

I mean using helicopters and TV cameras and such things, instead of keeping the policeman on the beat, where he belongs.

Now you have a question you can answer.

You will often receive such obscure questions. The questioner knows what he wants to ask, but is not used to speaking in public. Finding himself on his feet, with a hundred people staring at him, he gets flustered and fails to make himself clear.

Under procedure 2, the chairman may or may not ask for clarification of obscure questions. If he does not you will have to do it.

Under procedure 3, the chairman usually lays aside meaningless questions and reads only the clear, sensible ones. (Another advantage of this procedure.)

5. Suppose a well-meaning member of the audience gets up, says a few rambling sentences, but poses no definite question. Don't snub him by saying, "I'm afraid I don't follow what you mean. Next question, please!"

Don't start him off again by asking, "Could you explain exactly what your question is please?"

He probably will be unable to explain; the "rambler" cannot be clear and concise.

The best way to deal with him is to pick on some word or phrase that he used, and say a few words about it, pleasantly. The rest of the audience has lost track of what he was saying, so they will be impressed at your ability to make something of it.

For example, after your speech on "New Methods In Education," a rambler gets up and says:

I've been very interested in what the speaker had to say about the many and various changes taking place in education. We would all agree that we live in changing times, and that education seems to be changing, too. When I was in school, we had none of the computers or closed circuit TV that they have today, and yet it's an open question whether we were any worse for it. There is certainly no point in change for the sake of change, and yet I would be the last one to stand in the way of genuine progress. I put it to you, Mr. Speaker, do you agree?

Under procedure 2, the chairman probably will not try to repeat this rigmarole, but will simply call on you to reply. Under procedure 1, you had better not try to repeat any part of it. There is not even anything here that you can ask him to define. You recognize him as a "rambler." So you pick on the word "Computers" and say something like this:

Yes, sir, you're quite right! Only a few years ago, a student graduating from high school could expect to use a pen and ink pot in his work, and live in a world run by pen-and-ink methods. So he was educated with a pen and ink pot. Nowadays, even if the school graduate doesn't actually use a computer, he will certainly have to live in a computer-using society. So it is only common sense to introduce him in school to the computer and its functions.

The rambler will feel pleased; he will think that he has asked a penetrating question and that you have answered him; and you have created an opportunity to say something significant to the audience.

6. You occasionally meet a questioner who, because of a strong foreign accent, a thick dialect or a speech impediment, is partly or wholly incomprehensible.

If you understand a few words, treat this questioner like the rambler. If you cannot understand anything he says, then the audience has not understood him, either. So invent a question in your own mind and give a brief answer.

The point is to avoid humiliating the questioner because of his difficulty with the language.

7. If the question is plain, give a plain answer. But don't slip into the habit of ending with "Does that answer your question?" "Does that satisfy you?" or "Have I cleared up that point now?" Such phrases invite the questioner to reply with a supplementary question, or perhaps to get into an argument with you.

8. Suppose a questioner says something that is wrong. Then don't anatagonize him by telling him he is wrong. *Concede something,* then lead smoothly and tactfully into an explanation of the truth.

For example, suppose I have been speaking on "Poetry Today." A questioner says, "Mr. Hull, wouldn't you agree that no sincere poet can make money writing poetry in a Philistine society such as ours?"

It would be tactless to reply, "I certainly wouldn't agree. Plenty of poets make money."

A better reply would be, "It may prove impossible for the poet to make money if he aims his writing at the Philistine part of society. Nevertheless, there are markets for poetry. Some of them pay well—a dollar a line and up. If the poet plans his marketing as carefully as his writing, he can make money.

9. If you receive a hostile question, keep your temper and answer politely.

10. If someone has made an absolute pest of himself—perhaps by interrupting the speech, or with repeated rude, hostile questions—you can deal with him more severely, *provided he has already lost the sympathy of the audience.*

Turn on him with a series of questions until you force him to admit ignorance on some point. Then say something like, "You don't know? *Then keep quiet!*"

Here is an imaginary example. Suppose the speech was on Adult Education in the Arts.

Pest: Mr. Speaker, you claim to teach so-called creative writing in night school. Now, be frank, isn't the whole night school system just a money-making racket for you and the other instructors? It's a well-known fact that art cannot be taught, that the artist is born, not made.

SPEAKER: Is it a well-known fact? Who knows it?

PEST: I do, and millions more.

SPEAKER: Name ten of them.

PEST: Er . . . ah . . .

SPEAKER: You can't. You don't know what you're talking about. So shut up and sit down.

Here is another example, following a speech in support of John Goodfellow, a candidate for mayor.

PEST: How do you have the nerve to ask us to vote for Goodfellow? Goodfellow is a crook.

SPEAKER: A crook? What did he do wrong?

PEST: He stole money.

SPEAKER: Where from?

PEST: From the firm he worked for.

SPEAKER: Are you sure of that?

PEST: Absolutely sure.

SPEAKER: (Taking out pen and notebook) Will you tell me your name, please?

PEST: What do you want to know my name for?

SPEAKER: To make an appointment with you. As soon as the meeting's over, we'll both go down to the Police Station, and you'll lay a charge of theft against John Goodfellow.

PEST: Er . . . well . . . I wouldn't want to do that.

SPEAKER: Why not?

PEST: I don't have the evidence.

SPEAKER: I thought not. You're shooting your mouth off, and you have no evidence to back it up. So sit down and keep quiet.

If you know more about your subject than the audience (and if you are well prepared, you will know more) you should have little difficulty in trapping any pest who tries to harass you. But I emphasize that this method should be used only if the pest obviously has not got the audience on his side.

11. If you don't know the answer to a question, admit it. "I'm

sorry, I don't know the answer to that." Don't dodge, don't invent. The audience will like you better for being frank.

12. If you know the answer, but don't want to reveal it, dodge the question. Begin as if you were going to answer it, but side step to a slightly different subject and talk forcefully and interestingly about that for a minute or two.

For example, after a political campaign speech in an agricultural district, you receive the question:

Mr. Speaker, isn't it a fact that your party is promising the city voters to hold food prices down? And isn't that another way of promising to hold farm incomes down?

You answer:

Food prices are a burning issue now, and will be for years to come. There are many elements that go into the cost of food by the time it's bought by the city consumer. Let's consider first the cost of production. As you know, a fertile piece of land, efficiently cultivated, will produce more wheat or corn or tomatoes or hogs at a lower cost per pound than a less fertile piece of land, less efficiently cultivated.

Then there's the question of transportation costs; to a large extent, those are governed by trade-union agreements that neither my party nor any other party can control. . . . etc.

Lead on to a brief discussion of the elements that affect food prices. If this is interesting and relevant to the listeners, most of them will not notice that you did not precisely answer the question.

13. Sometimes a questioner asks you something that you have already explained in your speech. Don't snub him: "If you had been listening earlier, you would have heard. . .etc."

Simply explain the point again briefly and, if possible, in different words, and with different examples or comparisons from those you used the first time. Some of the audience will recognize that you had dealt with the matter earlier; many will not. Welcome such questions; they give you extra opportunities to drive home important points.

Interruptions from the Audience

You may sometimes have to cope with interruptions of various kinds. Here are some hints that will be helpful.

Late-Comers

Late-comers can be a nuisance during the early part of a meeting, but there is not much you can do about them. Most of them are late by accident. They come in as quietly as they can, and tiptoe to a seat.

Don't pause in your speech, or you will lose the attention of the audience. Don't make any comment that would humiliate the late-comers. Why arouse their enmity? Your job is to make the audience feel well-disposed toward you.

If necessary, speak a little more loudly and more slowly to overcome the disturbance produced by late-comers.

Crying Infants

Ignore the noise if it is mild and intermittent. If it becomes loud and sustained, ask the mother politely to take the child out.

"Madam would you mind taking the baby out for a few minutes, please, for the comfort of the rest of the audience?"

The phrase about the comfort of the audience softens any resentment that your request might arouse.

Restless Audience

Restlessness produces wriggling, foot-shuffling and coughing. It is usually due to one of five causes.

1. They are too hot or too cold. If they are too hot, women will be shrugging their coats off, men trying to loosen their ties. People will begin to fan themselves with programs, if they have them. Some people will yawn; others may doze off to sleep.

If they are too cold, people will huddle into their coats and hunch their shoulders.

Don't fight needlessly against unfavorable temperatures. Pause and ask the chairman if the heat can be turned up, or the windows opened, to provide a comfortable temperature.

2. They cannot hear you. Some people will have their heads cocked in a strained "listening" attitude. Speak louder and more slowly, and articulate more distinctly.

3. They are bored because you are going too slowly for them— not necessarily speaking too slowly, but dealing with your material too slowly, so that they have understood and grasped it while you are still laboring with more explanations, proofs and examples. Yawning, looking around the room and out the windows, wriggling, shuffling and whispering, are the signs to watch for. Skip some of the explanations, and cover the ground as quickly as they can follow you.

4. They are puzzled because you are going too fast for them— not necessarily speaking too fast, but not explaining the material fully enough. They cannot understand, so they get bored. You can detect this condition because some of them will wear a recognizable puzzled look—a slight frown and wrinkled brow. Give more explanations, proofs and examples, so that each point is understood, and you carry the audience along with you.

5. They are bored by your monotonous delivery. This, of course, should not happen. But if you see it has, immediately use more variety of pace, pitch, power and tone, give more expression to your face, and use more gestures.

Talking In the Audience

You may sometimes find that, although most of the audience are interested and silent, a couple of people, out of sheer rudeness, will carry on a conversation loudly enough to disturb others.

Here are two counter-measures. First, try a *sudden, brief* increase of power, combined with a sharp look at the talkers. If this does not silence them, stop speaking *in the middle of a sentence* and stand silent, glaring at the talkers. This will draw upon them the attention of the whole audience, and they will usually subside.

Laughter

If you say something funny, try not to laugh with the audience. Laughing makes you breathless. It also hinders you in the sharp observation of the audience that you need in order to get the best effect. Proceed as follows:

1. As the laugh begins and swells, *don't move.* Stand stock-still, smiling, watching the audience.

2. Don't try to speak over the laughter.

3. Listen carefully to the volume of the laughter. It will rise to a peak, then begin to decline.

4. Don't wait for the laughter to die naturally, but when it has declined about half-way from its peak toward zero, *move, and draw in a breath.* The audience will immediately hush, and you can continue. The move can be very small; a slight raising of the head, a movement of your notes, a quick parting of the lips, a short step forward—almost anything will do.

This technique is important. Practice it; master it. It leaves the audience feeling they would like to have laughed a little more, and that is precisely what you want them to feel. It makes each subsequent laugh easier to obtain. Whereas if you let them laugh themselves into silence the first time, it will be harder to arouse their laughter again a little later on.

Applause

If you draw applause during your speech, handle it as you handle laughter. When it has half-subsided, check it with a movement and a breath, and continue.

Applause at the end of a speech, naturally, can be allowed to continue unchecked.

Practical Jokers

You may have a so-called friend in the audience who tries to disturb you by making funny faces or gestures, or by holding up something that he thinks will embarrass you or make you laugh.

Don't look at him. Keep your gaze moving over other parts of the audience, but don't let it settle on the joker.

If he becomes very annoying, treat him like a talker; stop in mid-sentence and glare at him.

If he still persists, ask the chairman to call him to order, for the comfort and convenience of the rest of the audience.

Hecklers

Usually you will encounter hecklers only at political meetings. Because of the strong passions involved, political speaking is rather difficult. Avoid it until you have gained considerable experience in less trying situations.

Still, here are some hints that will help you face hecklers confidently and effectively.

1. Don't be afraid. Remember that you have the advantage. The audience has come to hear you, not to hear the heckler. You are on the platform, above the audience and facing them. He is on the floor, level with the audience; he has his back to some of them, and the others necessarily have their backs to him. If you are using a microphone, your advantage over the heckler is much greater.

2. Don't sacrifice your advantage. Don't engage in arguments with a heckler; in doing this you dignify him with the status of a debating opponent. Don't invite him to come up to the platform or to the microphone.

3. At the first interruption, reply with something like this: "If you have anything to say, sir, please save it for the question period at the end of the meeting."

4. If further interruptions are not too troublesome, simply ignore them. Speak louder and more distinctly and keep hammering your points home to the audience.

5. If the interruptions become too tiresome, get tough with him. For example:

"Is there a ventriloquist in the house? Your dummy is out of control."

"Why don't you keep your mouth shut? Your brains are running out."

(To a drunken heckler) "Why don't you go back to the saloon and get them to put a head on you?"

(Addressed to the audience, with a gesture toward the heckler) "Empty vessels make most noise."

When dealing with a heckler, keep calm, keep smiling. If he makes you lose your temper, he has won. If you get the audience laughing at his expense, you have won.

Bad Acoustics

Moderate resonance in a hall helps the speaker, but a loud, prolonged echo can be a nuisance; so can a "dead" room in which there is little or no resonance.

As a rule, the greater the area of smooth, hard surface on floor, walls, ceiling and furnishings, the louder echo the room will produce. In a big, bare room, the echo has far to travel; at some points in the audience the echo of one syllable arrives just in time to interfere with the hearing of the next syllable the speaker utters. School gymnasiums, for example, often have a clattering, troublesome echo.

On the other hand, carpets, drapes, padded furniture and sound absorbent ceiling tiles reduce echo. The bodies and clothes of an audience absorb sound. A room that, when empty, has little echo may, when full of people, sound distressingly dead. The speaker's voice seems small, distant and unimpressive.

If you have not spoken in a hall before, try to test your voice on the platform before the meeting. You can hear fairly well whether it sounds dead or alive, and if there is a strong echo.

If you have to speak from a proscenium-type stage, with an arched opening across which the curtain moves, you may find that your placement on the stage makes an enormous difference to the transmission of your voice. If you are too far back from the edge of the platform, your voice may rise up and get lost behind the proscenium. If you move a few feet nearer to the audience, you may find that your voice travels strongly and easily out over the auditorium.

If you cannot make a preliminary trial, carefully observe speakers who precede you. See where they stand, how they direct their voices, and what is the result.

To overcome the effect of a dead room, use more power, more variety, more facial expression and more gestures.

To overcome an echo, speak more slowly, and take special care with articulation.

Note any changes in the sound of your voice that result from turning, raising or lowering your head as you speak. If a certain head position produces a particularly bad echo, avoid it for the rest of your speech. If one position produces particularly clear sound, favor that position.

Noises

You will sometimes be bothered by the sound of police, fire or ambulance sirens, truck or airplane motors, air drills and such things. The noise will distract some of the listeners yet, if you stop, you lose the attention of all the audience. Moreover, they lose the thread of your speech. You will have to make an effort to help them gather their thoughts together when you resume. Review briefly what you were saying, and then lead them on again. If you can with any reasonable effort continue, do so. Increase your power, reduce your pace, and articulate perfectly.

But if the noise makes your voice inaudible, or completely distracts the audience—for example, aircraft passing low overhead—don't try to fight it. Simply pause until it subsides. Then proceed as suggested above; review the point you were making before the interruption and continue.

If the noise is bad, but is controllable—for example, workmen or music elsewhere in the building—ask the chairman, with a smile, if it can be stopped, *for the comfort of the audience.*

Obstructions

Sometimes you find a big pot of flowers, or some other obstruction, right in front of you. It may hide your face, or the upper part of your body, from some of the audience. Ask the chairman to have it removed. Every member of the audience should be able to see you clearly. A head-and-shoulders view is not enough. Your torso and arms must be visible so that you can gesture effectively.

Summary

Be sure the audience hears the question before you answer it. Listen only to the questioner; reply to the whole audience.

Deal diplomatically with incomprehensible questions.

Don't argue with questioners.

Crush a pest—question him until he cannot answer.

If you don't know the answer, admit it.

Dodge a dangerous question by changing the subject.

Don't pause for late-comers.

Ask to have a crying infant removed.

Restless audience:

1. Too hot, too cold—get temperature modified.
2. Audience cannot hear—speak louder and slower.
3. Bored—cover the ground faster.
4. Puzzled—explain more fully.
5. Monotonous delivery—vary pace, pitch, power, tone.

Don't tolerate talking in the audience.

Handling laughter:

1. Don't laugh. Smile. Stand still.
2. Keep quiet.
3. Listen for the laughter to decline.
4. Move, inhale—laughter stops. Continue.

Handle applause the same way as laughter.

Don't tolerate practical jokers.

Handling hecklers:

1. Don't be afraid.
2. Don't argue with hecklers.
3. Ignore mild interruptions.
4. Be harsh with stubborn hecklers.

In an acoustically dead room, use more power, variety, expression.

In an echoing room, speak slowly; articulate carefully.

Try to overcome extraneous noises.

Don't let obstructions hide you from the audience.

Exercises

1. Let each speaker answer questions from other members of the class.

2. Let other members of the class heckle the speaker and so accustom him to carry on in face of opposition.

3. Try to get experience speaking in rooms of widely differing acoustic quality.

20. Chairmanship

Order is Heaven's first law.

ALEXANDER POPE

Anyone who is known as a speaker is sooner or later invited to be a chairman at meetings. The chairman, although his duties are not arduous, is largely responsible for the success or failure of the meeting. Bad chairmanship can ruin the effect of good speeches; a good chairman can make the most of a roster of mediocre speakers. Here are some hints that will help you to chair meetings easily and effectively.

Preliminary Arrangements

The chairman is responsible either for introducing the speaker to the audience, or for getting someone else to do it. Don't wait until five minutes before the start of the meeting, then button-hole a member of your organization and say, "By the way, Bill, I'd like you to say a few words of introduction before Mr. Demosthenes speaks."

This is hard on Bill, and not fair to the speaker. So arrange introductions well in advance.

The chairman also must either thank the speaker, or arrange in advance for someone else to do it.

If there are several speakers on the program, the chairman should know, or find out, their relative merits and plan his program so as to produce the best possible effect. The poorest speaker

194

should go first and the others in ascending order of merit, with the best speaker last.

Let each speaker know, well in advance, how long he is required to speak.

I was once lecturing to a historical society, and had been told to prepare an hour's speech. After thirty minutes the chairman passed me a note: "We usually have an intermission for refreshments half-way through. Coffee is ready. Please stop now and resume afterwards."

If there is any unusual arrangement of the program, tell the speaker *in advance,* so he can prepare.

Tell each speaker, too, what other speakers, if any, are to be on the platform. Tell him if there is to be a question period or discussion following the speech.

As chairman, you should dress quietly, so as not to distract attention from the speakers.

Be sure you have pen and paper; you may need to write some notes during the meeting.

The Hall and Platform

It is a good idea to inspect the hall before the audience arrives. See that lighting, heating and ventilation are working properly. If the audience is too hot or too cold, or cannot see the speaker clearly, they will be restless; and your job of controlling the meeting will be harder than it need be.

Also, before the audience arrives, see that everything is ready on the platform. Check chairs, tables, lecterns; see that there are glasses and water for speakers. Some speakers get nervous if the water is not in sight, even though they may not use it.

If the speaker wants a blackboard, see that chalk and eraser are provided. If a projection screen is required, see that it is properly set up.

Check that there is enough light for the speaker to read his notes.

Arrange the chairs as you want them, and decide where each person will sit.

Neglect of these seemingly simple precautions can cause delays and embarrassment during the meeting. A good chairman attends to them in person and so ensures a smoothly running meeting.

Dealing with Speakers

Before the Meeting

Be at the hall early and greet the speaker when he arrives. After preliminary courtesies, remind him of the arrangements. Tell him at what point on the program he is to speak; for how long; who else is on the program; and arrangements for intermission, questions, discussion, refreshments, etc.

Offer to give the speaker a time-signal to tell him when he has five and two minutes to go. (He should be able to control the length of his own speech and finish within a minute of the allotted time, but many speakers cannot do this, and are glad of the chairman's aid.)

A convenient five-minute signal is to fold your arms, and display the thumb and four fingers on the side toward the speaker. Similarly displaying two fingers is the two-minute signal. Or you can display the fingers by laying a hand on the table, on your knee, or otherwise putting it into the speaker's range of vision.

The thing to avoid is letting the speaker turn and ask, "Mr. Chairman, how much longer have I got?" This is a severe disruption of any speech.

Don't drag the speaker into a discussion of his subject. He might prefer to have a few minutes' peace, to rest, glance over his notes and collect his thoughts. Offer to arrange this. If he accepts, get him off into a corner and keep other people from pestering him. Tell them that, if they want to talk to the speaker, they can do so after the meeting.

Some speakers, however, enjoy talking about the subject in advance; they find that it stimulates their thinking. If your speaker wants to do this, lead him on to talk as much as he likes.

It is part of your duty to set the speaker at ease and bring him to the platform ready to give of his best. So *don't press liquor on the speaker!* Don't let other people do so. It is a bad omen if the speaker demands liquor before the speech. If you must give it to him, at least try to hold his consumption to a minimum.

Two minutes before starting time, call the platform party

together. Tell them what positions they will occupy on stage. Let the main speaker go on to the platform first. Other people should follow in such an order that they can reach their seats without too much dodging around. The chairman should go on last.

On the Platform

When the platform party is seated, begin the meeting. Every minute's delay is a minute slashed from the speaker's time; he will not thank you for it.

Make *a few* preliminary remarks, welcoming the audience and explaining whatever needs explaining about the purpose of the meeting. In these remarks, take care to set the correct *tone* for the occasion.

For example, don't lead off with a string of well-told jokes, get the audience roaring with laughter, and then introduce a speaker who is to appeal for funds for war orphans. Or, just before calling on a humorous speaker, don't pay a moving tribute to the president of your organization who has just died after long suffering, leaving a widow and four small children.

After your introductory remarks, brief and in the correct tone, introduce the first speaker, or call on the person who is to do it.

"It gives me great pleasure to call upon Mr. Joe Doakes, who is to introduce our first speaker."

While any speaker is on his feet, the chairman should look at him, not gaze around the audience. Look at the audience only if something occurs that requires your intervention.

Don't whisper to other people on the platform, or pass notes back and forth, except in an emergency. Such antics tend to distract attention from the speaker.

Glance at your watch occasionally, and give the agreed time-signals when they are due.

When a speaker finishes, it is appropriate for the chairman to lead the applause, meanwhile smiling and continuing to look at the speaker.

Long-Winded Speakers

You may have trouble with a speaker who goes on too long, ignoring your time-signals. Or perhaps he said he did not need time-signals, then proves unable to time himself. If, at the end of the allotted time, he shows no sign of being nearly finished, write a note: "Five minutes more, please." Put it on lectern or table where he cannot help seeing it.

If he is still talking after five minutes, give him another note: "Two minutes more, please."

If this does not stop him, try a third note: "Please finish at once."

As a last resort, stand up and interrupt him. Say something like this. "Ladies and Gentlemen, I'm sorry to interrupt Mr. Demosthenes, but time is pressing, and I know you are eager to hear the other speakers on our program. Thank you, Mr. Demosthenes." Lead the audience in applause.

Such emergency measures should, of course, be used with discretion. If your main speaker obviously has the adience spellbound, it would be silly to hold him to a time-limit. But if a preliminary speaker, or one speaker in a debate or panel discussion, is long-winded and dull, the chairman must be ruthless to save the meeting from failure.

Cutting off a tedious speaker will make him your enemy, but it will make everyone else in the hall your friend.

Stay On the Platform

Some chairmen slip down into the audience as soon as the main speaker has started. True, the chairman gets a better view of the speaker from the floor of the hall; but his place is on the platform, to keep control of the meeting. Suppose the lights fail, someone faints, fire breaks out, or someone creates a disturbance; the chairman must be on the platform to deal promptly with such emergencies.

Brevity

In all you say as chairman, *be brief*. A long-winded chairman is an absolute nuisance. Your job as chairman is not to compete with the speakers, but to aid and encourage them. So keep your own remarks short, and make it abundantly clear to auxiliary speakers (those who introduce and thank the main speakers) that they, too, must be brief.

It is better for the meeting to be too short than too long. Send the audience away wanting more.

Dealing with the Audience

Small Audience

If you have a small audience—less than half the capacity of the hall—it's a good idea to get the listeners massed together at the front of the hall before the meeting begins. They will be nearer to the speaker and will be able to see and hear better, and they will be closer to each other. This helps them achieve strong emotional reactions so that they will enjoy the speeches more. Also it prevents them from seeing the empty seats which would remind them of the small attendance.

Merely asking the audience to come to the front may fail to move them; and thus you will have lost control of the meeting before it begins. Here is an easy, effective way to do it.

1. *Don't* begin with a comment on the "disappointing" size of the audience. *Don't* offer excuses for the small turnout. Begin by saying, with a smile, "Ladies and Gentlemen, will everyone who can see an empty seat anywhere in front of him please raise his right hand?" Raise your own right hand to set the example.

2. When the hands are raised, say: "Thank you. Now, everyone who has raised his hand, please stand up." Make an upsweeping gesture with both hands as they rise. Keep smiling.

3. When they are standing, say: "Thank you. Now, all you who are standing, please move down toward the platform and fill up the front rows of seats."

4. When all are seated, continue: "Thank you. Now we can all see each other much more clearly."

5. Proceed to your preliminary remarks.

(If you have music available, play a lively march, beginning the very moment you conclude remark No. 3, and ending when all are seated again.)

Talkative Audience

As chairman, you are the first person to address the audience. Usually they become quiet if you stand and say, loudly and clearly, "Ladies and Gentlemen."

If that does not quiet them, here is a trick that will. Begin talking, *rather softly,* addressing yourself *to the front three rows of people*. The others will soon stop chattering, out of curiosity to hear what you are saying.

This is better than shouting "Quiet, please!"

If people keep talking during a speech, the speaker should quiet them. (This is explained in Chapter 19.) But if he does not or cannot do this, and if the talkers are disturbing the rest of the audience, the chairman must intervene.

1. Stand and move to the speaker.

2. Wait until he ends a sentence. Say, "Mr. Demosthenes, pardon me if I interrupt you for a moment."

3. Look sternly at the talkers. Point at them, with arm fully extended, index finger straight. Say: "Will those people who are carrying on a conversation please show a little consideration for the rest of the audience. Keep quiet, please, and let the speaker continue with no more interruption."

4. Turn to the speaker with a smile. "Thank you, Mr. Demosthenes. Please go on."

5. Return quietly to your chair.

Serious Disturbances

If members of the audience make so much noise that the speaker cannot be heard, and if they do not subside at your request, order the ushers to put them out of the hall.

If violence occurs, or is threatening, tell someone to call the police, meanwhile instructing the ushers to preserve order as best they can.

Question Time

Properly controlled, the question period can be the most interesting and instructive part of the meeting.

If questions are to be spoken from the floor, there is sometimes an embarrassing silence at the beginning of the question period, because nobody wants to speak first. The meeting seems to fall flat; the chairman has to plead for questions.

Guard against such embarrassment by preparing a question yourself during the speech. Announce the question period; wait three seconds and, if no one has spoken, say, "There's one question that I'd like to ask the speaker. What is the reason for...etc?"

A better plan is to arrange with two reliable members of the audience to prepare questions and to ask them promptly at the start of the question period.

Spoken questions from the floor should not be addressed to the speaker, but to the chair: "Mr. Chairman, I would like to ask the speaker, etc."

This indirect method of questioning tends to prevent arguments between questioners and speaker.

If the audience is small, and a questioner speaks loudly enough to be heard by everyone, wait until he finishes, then smile and look at the speaker as a sign for him to answer. But if you think that some of the audience did not hear the question, repeat it. "The questions is...etc." Then look at the speaker as before.

If one of the audience tries to monopolize the question period by asking many questions, or trying to make a speech, suppress him. "Now, sir, you've had your turn. Please let other members of the audience ask their questions."

With spoken questions, people usually raise their hands, or stand, to indicate their desire to ask a question. Try to take their questions in the order in which they gave the signal. If several people signaled at once, take them in random order. Don't take all the questions from one part of the hall in succession. Take first from one side, then the other, from the front, then from the back. This helps to sustain the interest of the audience. Even if someone has not asked a question himself, he feels a particular interest in a question asked by someone near him.

Be clear when you indicate who is to ask his question; point at the person and say, "Yes, Sir?"

If two or more would-be questioners are so close that pointing alone will not distinguish them, add a descriptive touch. "Next question: the gentleman in the brown suit, please."

If questions are submitted in writing, sort them out to avoid duplication. If possible, let the speaker see the questions before you read them, so that he has time to think of his answers. Read each question loudly and slowly, then hand the paper to the speaker and let him make his answer.

Close the question period decisively when time is up, or earlier if it begins to flag. Don't try to prolong it by pleading for more questions.

Then either thank the speaker yourself, or call on the person who is to do it.

Impartiality

The chairman customarily speaks, not for himself, but as a representative of the organization that arranged the meeting. In case of disputes or difficulties, use an impersonal form of speech.

"The chair rules so-and-so. . ."

"Please address your questions to the chair, not to the speaker."

"Please show some respect for the chair."

"That is for the chair to decide."

This style of speech tends to ruffle people's feelings less than the frequent use of "I."

For chairing business meetings, get a copy of the procedural rules of the organization. Make yourself familiar with them. Take a copy to the meeting, so you can authoritatively quote the appropriate rule in settling disputes.

Summary

Arrange introductions and thanks for speakers in advance.

Put the best speaker last on the program.

Inform speakers of your program arrangements.

Inspect hall and platform before speakers arrive.

Offer to give the speaker a time signal.

Put the speaker at ease before the meeting begins.

Begin the meeting on time.

Don't distract the audience's attention from the speaker.

Tactfully yet firmly control long-winded speakers.

Stay on the platform.

In your capacity as chairman, be brief.

Move a small audience to the front of the hall.

Keep control of the meeting at all times.

Get the question period moving briskly.

Don't let the question period die a slow death.

In your conduct as chairman be impersonal, be impartial.

21. Microphones, Radio and Television

All the apparatus of the system, and its varied working . . .

LORD BROUGHAM

You will not make many speeches before you come face to face with a microphone. In a radio or TV studio, you need not worry about the functioning of the apparatus, but in public halls, microphones and other sound equipment vary from excellent to useless.

Public address systems vary so much that there are no fixed rules for using them. Still, here are some hints that can be helpful.

On the Platform

Microphones are installed in many places where they are not needed. I have seen a speaker using a microphone to address forty people in a room twenty feet square. I saw an amplifier giving continual trouble at a banquet of four hundred diners. It ruined three speeches with its booming, whistling and crackling. At last the chairman put down the microphone and said, "Can you hear me without this thing?"

"Yes," shouted the audience.

From then on, the oratory became a pleasure instead of a punishment.

There is no need to use a microphone for an audience of forty, or four hundred. Any speaker—man or woman—with a well-developed voice can address two thousand people without a microphone. In pre-microphone days, speakers used to make themselves heard by crowds of ten thousand, in the open air!

You will sometimes have the choice of using, or not using, a microphone; I would suggest that you never use it if you can do without it.

There are five disadvantages to using a microphone:

1. The apparatus is likely to depersonalize your voice to some extent.

2. If the microphone is too big, or is fixed too high, it hides part of your face.

3. The microphone ties you down; it restricts the movements of head, hands, arms and body that a speaker needs to make if his speech is to have its best effect. Admittedly, with the best microphones, you have some freedom to move without getting out of range. But with the average-to-poor instrument on the average platform, head movements of more than a few inches produce unpleasant changes of volume. The result is a "frozen speaker," afraid to move head, arms or body, and thus robbed of a useful means of emphasis and expression.

4. You can never rely on an amplifier. It may work well for a while then suddenly fail. Your speech is disrupted while the chairman scurries around to find what is wrong and to have it adjusted.

5. A shining, nickel-plated microphone or microphone stand distracts the gaze of the audience from your face. The spectator's eye tends to seek the brightest object within its field of view, and that gleaming piece of metal is brighter than your face.

In some conditions, a microphone is useful:

1. When you must address a vast audience in a hall with bad acoustics, or when your voice must be carried to an overflow audience in another room.

2. When a sore throat prevents you from developing normal vocal power.

3. When your speech, as well as being heard by the audience in the hall, must be broadcast or recorded.

Otherwise, speak without a microphone. Get it removed before the meeting begins, or some spectators will keep looking at it and wondering why you are not using it.

There is an exception to this rule: If you are one of several speakers on the program, and if preceding speakers have used the microphone, follow their example. The audience now has the idea that a speaker must use the microphone to be audible, and even if they can hear you, they will think they cannot.

If you must use a microphone, these hints will minimize your difficulties.

1. If, as chairman, you are unfamiliar with the microphone, try it out, before the audience arrives, with a friend sitting at the back of the hall to tell you how your voice sounds. When the meeting begins, you will be the first to speak into the instrument. For best results, you should know that it is working, and know how close to it, and how loudly, you need to speak. It creates a poor impression if the chairman has to open a meeting by counting, or snapping his fingers, into the microphone and shouting, "Is this thing working?"

2. As chairman, note in advance the "on" and "off" positions of the switches on amplifier and microphone standard. Be *sure* at the start of the meeting that the microphone is switched on. Even if you checked it beforehand, some meddler may have flipped the switch without your knowing it.

I attended a political meeting where the main speaker, a federal cabinet minister, was inaudible to most of the audience. Thinking that the microphone was switched on, he spoke at conversational volume. When question-time came, he found that the microphone had been switched off throughout his speech. He promptly turned it on, but the damage was done!

3. As a speaker, if you see that the microphone is too high or too low for you, get the chairman to adjust it *before you begin to speak*. If you start with the microphone too high, it hides part of your face; if it is too low, you must stoop to it. If you begin like this, you must either stop to adjust the microphone, and so break the flow of your speech, or you must struggle with the microphone while you speak, thus diverting the audience's attention from what you are saying.

And your struggle may be in vain; you may not be able to move the microphone or, having moved it, you may be unable to lock it in the new position. In either event, you make yourself ridiculous in the eyes of the audience.

If anyone is to look ridiculous, let it be the chairman, not you. Stand at the microphone as he adjusts it. Have it placed so that the audience can see your entire face over the top of it. Don't let it hide your mouth. The audience needs to see your lip movements as an aid to comprehension of your words and emotions.

4. Keep your hands off the microphone and its mounting. Some speakers, using a floor-based standard microphone, cling to the

upright rod like drowning men to a lifeline. Any contact with the microphone may produce unwanted noise. Even if it does not do that, it makes you look nervous.

5. Don't stick your face close to the microphone and speak softly. You will be heard all right, but you run the risk of speaking much too fast, and of slipping into a conversational style that fails to convey your meaning and feelings to a large audience.

It is better to stand about eighteen inches from the microphone and speak fairly loudly—as you would to an audience of fifty people without amplification. This helps you to use, easily and effectively, the techniques that you have practiced without a microphone. The microphone is there to aid you, not to do all your work for you.

To measure your distance, stand with an elbow touching your side, raise the forearm to the horizontal, with finger extended. Your middle finger should just touch the microphone standard.

6. Keep at a constant distance from the microphone. Don't sway to and fro; don't walk about the platform. *Don't turn your head* to address remarks to the chairman or to other speakers.

7. Remember to keep looking at and speaking to *the audience,* not the microphone. If the light is brighter on the microphone than on the audience, you are tempted to focus your eyes, thoughts and voice on the instrument. Resist the temptation. As far as you can, forget the microphone, and keep projecting your gaze, thoughts and feelings, toward your listeners.

8. With a microphone, articulation is particularly important. Some sound systems are weak on high frequencies, so you will have to emphasize those frequencies more than usual to compensate. Practice this at home, with a tape recording. Stand eighteen inches from the microphone; speak, record, play back and correct yourself until you develop perfect articulation.

9. Sound systems sometimes develop a condition called "feedback." The microphone picks up the sound from the loudspeakers and feeds it back into the amplifier, along with the speaker's voice. This makes a howling or whistling sound. You can sometimes stop it by placing the palm of your hand gently over the microphone. If this does not work, or if feedback occurs repeatedly, ask the chairman to have the amplifier adjusted.

If anything else goes wrong, appeal promptly to the chairman. It is no use struggling on, fighting a malfunctioning or maladjusted sound system.

10. Microphones and amplifiers vary widely in sensitivity, selectivity and power. You can get valuable guidance, if you are not the first speaker on the program, by closely watching preceding speakers. Notice how they use their voices, and how the apparatus responds to them. See what goes right and what goes wrong, and modify your tactics accordingly.

Radio

Radio broadcasting is radically different from platform speaking. Some techniques that are essential in an auditorium are obnoxious in the studio. That is because on radio, although you may be addressing fifty thousand people, *you are not addressing a crowd*. The listeners are sitting, by ones and twos, in their homes or automobiles.

Your relationship to them is not that of orator to audience, but that of *guest to host*. They have not come to a hall to hear you; they have invited you (by turning a switch) into their company and if you do not behave courteously and pleasantly they will, by the same process, turn you out.

As you speak, you are not fifty feet away from them, high on a platform but—as they hear you—you are a few feet away, with your mouth on a level with their ears.

There is no crowd effect between members of the radio audience, no communication of emotions from one listener to another.

They cannot see you so gestures and body movements will not help to convey your meaning.

So to fit these conditions, radio speaking demands a quiet voice, a fairly rapid pace, and a conversational style.

(One exception: If a platform speech is being broadcast, your prime duty is to the audience in the hall. Use regular public speaking technique. The radio audience will understand the circumstances.)

Here are some hints that will help to make radio speaking easy for you and enjoyable for your listeners.

Voice

1. *Power*. Forget about the power and projection you developed for platform work; speak with the same power you use in

conversation. You are usually sitting: this reminds you not to use your standup oratorical power.

Avoid monotony; some increases and decreases of power, within the conversational range, add a pleasing variety to your voice.

2. *Pitch.* Most home radio receivers are grossly deficient in reproducing low frequencies. So your voice, as it reaches the listener, sounds *much higher in pitch* than it does to you and to other people in the studio.

Allow for this distortion by speaking *considerably lower* than your ordinary conversational pitch. Women, should lower their voices down toward the contralto range, men, toward the bass. Rehearsal with a tape recorder will help you make this pitch-change at will, and to sustain it as long as you need to. Work on this point; it will make a great difference to your radio speaking.

Here, too, avoid monotony. Use frequent variations of pitch, while keeping within the lower range you have set for yourself.

3. *Pace.* If you speak as slowly as you do on the platform, you will sound hesitant and boring to radio listeners. About 150 words a minute is a fair pace. Time yourself, reading passages with known word counts into a tape recorder, and get the feel of going at 150 words a minute.

But don't maintain a constant pace. Less important words and phrases should be skimmed over quickly and lightly; more important ones should be delivered slowly.

4. *Expression.* Although gestures are meaningless on radio, facial expression is important, because changes in expression produce changes in the tone of your voice.

Let your face be mobile, then—even more mobile than for platform speaking. Make yourself *feel* as you speak, let your face express what you feel, and your voice will become expressive, too.

5. *Articulation.* Since your lips are unseen, articulation is even more important than in platform speaking.

Apparatus

You need not concern yourself with the microphone and other apparatus. Before the broadcast begins, someone will show you where to sit or stand in relation to the microphone. Your voice will be tested for volume, and the apparatus will be adjusted accordingly. Just maintain your position, and keep your voice in the conversational range of power.

Timing

Most radio broadcasts are timed fairly closely. If you are speaking without a script—being interviewed, or speaking in a panel discussion, for example—someone else will be responsible for timing the show. Ask whoever is in charge of timing what signals he will use as the show draws near its end. Be sure you understand the signals, and *follow them precisely*. Radio people loathe the speaker who won't stop talking when he should. They can cut you off, to be sure, but it is better for you to come to a graceful conclusion and have the show rounded off in the proper way.

After you have finished, *keep your mouth shut*. Don't blurt out remarks such as, "Well, that went off better than I expected," "Thank goodness that's over," or "Was I ever nervous! I thought I was going to collapse!"

The microphone may still be alive, transmitting your comments to the listening thousands!

So, after the show is over, keep still and say nothing until the words and actions of the staff clearly indicate that it is safe to relax.

Writing a Radio Script

For a solo broadcast, you may have to prepare and read a script, so that the station knows what you are going to say, and so that you can time your talk precisely. Here are some hints on writing and delivering a scripted radio talk.

Your talk should *not* sound as if it is being read off a script, but as if you were speaking impromptu. So the script must be colloquial, not literary, in style.

If at first you find it hard to write colloquially, this trick will help you. First prepare notes on the subject, as if you were going to make a speech. Then, guided by your notes, talk conversationally into a tape recorder. Play back what you have said and type it out. This should give you a useful basis for your script.

Timing the Radio Script

You will know, before beginning work on the script, the time your talk is supposed to run. When you are satisfied with the style of the script, check it for length. Get a watch with a second hand and read the script at the pace, and with the expression and pauses, that you will use on the air.

With a pencil, write in the margin of the script an appropriate number (1.00, 2.00, 3.00, 4.00, etc.) to mark the point you reach at the end of each minute.

Probably the first draft of the script will not be exactly the right length. So you must adjust it.

Suppose it is too short—say, by thirty seconds. From the time-marked script, calculate how many lines you deliver in thirty seconds. Then you will know how much extra material to write.

Suppose it is too long—say, it runs on eight lines beyond the cut-off point. Then cut eight lines from the script.

An addition or a cut, of course, need not be made in a solid chunk at the end of the script. The material can be added or removed piecemeal throughout the script, so that there are no noticeable gaps or patches.

After these adjustments, time the script again; it should come out right. Practice reading it, guided by the watch and time marks, until you achieve a uniformly accurate timing.

When you go to the studio to deliver the talk, the final script will have the time marks in the margin. (Take two carbon copies to hand to the producer and technician if they want them. These copies need not have the time marks.)

Every radio studio has a clock with a big sweep second hand. Ask to be placed in sight of the clock, so that you can time your reading. When you get the signal to start, note the position of the second hand on the clock. Glance at the clock frequently, as you pause in your reading, and compare the passage of time with the rate of your progress through the script. If you are getting ahead of your time marks, slow down; if you are lagging, speed up. Keep watching clock and time marks, and you should be able to keep to the pace you have planned and rehearsed, and finish very close to the assigned time.

Accuracy on timing tends to make you popular with radio producers and technicians.

Handling the Radio Script

Studio microphones are sensitive. Sounds of rustling or crackling paper will be picked up and broadcast. Soft paper, such as the kind sold for use in stencil duplicators, is suitable. It takes typescript clearly, and with care, you can handle it silently.

Don't pin, staple or bind the pages of your script together. Don't turn them over as you finish reading them.

If you are sitting at a table, lay the script on its surface; don't hold it in your hand. As you finish reading each page, *gently* lift it by one edge (don't slide it) and lay it aside, exposing the next page.

If you are standing at a lectern, gently lift each page as it is done with, and drop it to the floor. The slight sound it makes on touching the floor is too far from the microphone to be picked up.

Expression In the Radio Script

In your private rehearsals, you will be looking for the most expressive way of reading your script. When you find some change of tone, some pause, some rise or fall of pitch that is effective, you can keep it by marking it on your script. Invent your own code of expression marks, and use it. For example, an upward sloping line over a phrase shows a rise of pitch; a downward sloping line shows falling pitch. Underlinings for emphasis, dashes between words to mark pauses, notes in the margin on facial expressions— smile, frown, etc.—ensure that the results of your practice are carried through to your performance.

Type the script double-spaced, to give room for these expression marks. The slight trouble of inventing and using them will be repaid by the extra confidence and polish that they give to your radio work.

Television

On television, as on radio, a quiet, conversational style is most effective. The sound section of the typical TV receiver is more efficient than the average home radio receiver, so in TV there is no particular need to lower the pitch of your voice. Nevertheless, don't be shrill or squeaky.

Your face is visible, of course, and its changing expressions help to convey your meaning to viewers. So let your face be mobile. Let it show what you are supposed to be feeling. And smile often.

In a TV interview you need not worry about the microphones. You may have a small microphone (hung around your neck) which will pick up your voice perfectly without your making any special effort. Or the microphone may be mounted on a long, pivoted boom. It is then the duty of the boom-man to keep it close to the speakers without letting it move into range of the camera.

A red light near the lens shows which camera is transmitting at any moment. But don't dodge around trying to face it. Simply keep talking, and let the cameraman get front or side shots at will.

Since, for much of the time, the audience will see only a close-up of your face, don't depend on gestures to convey any part of your meaning. Depend instead on the expressive voice—meaningful changes of pace, pitch, power and tone—and on the expressive face.

As in radio, be sure what signals are used to indicate the passage of time. Ask about them, watch for them, and obey them.

Here, too, after you finish, *keep still, keep quiet,* and *keep smiling.* For all you know, they may be superimposing the closing titles over a close-up of your face. If you start tearing off the neck-microphone, or loosening your shirt collar, the effect is spoiled. Wait in your place until the studio director or technician comes forward to clearly indicate that all is over.

Summary

Don't use a microphone unless you need it.
Hints for using a microphone:
1. Try out the microphone before the meeting.
2. Be sure it is switched on.
3. Don't have it too high or too low.
4. Keep your hands off it.
5. Get 18 inches away from it, and speak fairly loudly.
6. Keep at a constant distance from it.
7. Look at the audience, not at the microphone.

8. Articulate carefully.
9. Don't struggle with malfunctions; ask the chairman to help.
10. See how other speakers use the microphone.

For radio work:

1. Use conversational power.
2. Use a low pitch.
3. Speak about 150 words a minute.
4. Let your face be expressive to get tonal variety.
5. Articulate carefully.
6. Be exact in your timing.
7. After you finish, keep your mouth shut.

Write radio scripts in conversational, not literary, style.

The radio script should be precisely timed.

Don't rustle the script as you use it.

In TV speaking, use a conversational style.

Exercise

On a subject of your choice, write a radio script that runs for ten minutes. Record it on tape, and check it for accuracy of timing.

22. Research

Few men make themselves masters of the things they write or speak.

JOHN SELDEN

Typically, the beginning speaker offers the audience nothing more than his own ideas on each subject. But unless you are a very important person, the audience is not much impressed with your ideas. To make a well-rounded, convincing speech, you must support those ideas with material from outside sources. To be a powerful speaker, you must know where to find the material you need —the material that will make you an *authority* on the subject.

Personal Investigation

If you are speaking about "Life on Mars," "Milton's Concept of Hell and Heaven," or "The Decline of the Roman Empire," you cannot visit the places, people and events in question. But for many subjects personal investigation is possible, and adds interest and authority to your speech. Here are some typical subjects with examples of personal investigations that could be made.

Alcoholism. Go to court and see the trials of a dozen or more cases of drunkenness and offenses triggered by drunkenness. Take notes.

Traffic Problems. Observe carefully, during a day's driving, all the hazards and problems you encounter; consider what could be done to reduce them. Stand for an hour at a busy intersection; and note what you see in the way of hazards, bad driving, etc.

Resource Conservation. Take a walk beside the nearest river, or go out into the country. Note how water, soil and vegetation are being affected by man's activities.

For most subjects, some kind of personal investigation is practicable. It need not be elaborate, time-consuming or costly, yet what you see and hear and experience will be more vivid and meaningful to you than what you read in books. Therefore, since you feel interested in it, you will find it easy to get the audience interested in it.

For instance, which of these two statements is more interesting?

Reports from the Regional Water Board indicate an ever-increasing pollution of our streams and rivers.

Or:

Last Saturday afternoon I walked for an hour beside Crystal Creek. Its water was covered with an iridescent film of oil. It smelled at one point of sulphur, at another of rotting garbage. I saw, floating on that creek, one old mattress, countless empty boxes and cartons, thick masses of some grayish scum that looked like dirty soapsuds, and one dead cat. And, let me remind you, that is the source from which our city draws its water supply.

Personal investigation, undeniably, adds vividness and power to the second statement.

So, whenever you can, investigate your subject in person and *take notes* as you go.

Formal Interviews

Another good source of information is the interview. The following hints will make interviewing easy and effective.

1. Find someone who is an authority on the subject. For "Life on Mars," an astronomer would be informative; for "Milton's Concept of Hell and Heaven," a Miltonian scholar and a theologian; for "The Decline of the Roman Empire," a historian. Make an appointment in advance, explaining clearly who you are, and what you want to talk about.

2. Prepare yourself with as much information as you can get

about the interviewee and the subject. You then can ask intelligent questions, understanding at once most of what the interviewee tells you, and avoid wasting his time and your own.

3. Don't be afraid. Most people enjoy talking about themselves and about their specialties; they are flattered to be intelligently interviewed.

4. An interview is wasted unless you take notes. Be sure of your equipment. Take two pens, in case one fails. Use a notebook with a stiff cover, so you can write on your knee, or while you are standing up.

5. Prepare a list of questions. Check them off as you get the answers. But don't confine yourself to the questions; try to get the expert talking freely. He knows, better than you do, what are the most important aspects of the subject.

6. If it is appropriate, ask the expert to show you any exhibits, photographs, etc. that he has; ask to see the scientist's laboratory, the manufacturer's factory, etc. This gives you a more vivid impression of the subject than you can get by sitting talking in a living room or office.

7. As soon as you can after the interview, review your notes, amplify anything that seems to be too brief, and jot down any further ideas that occur to you as a result of the interview.

Informal Interviews

On questions of general interest, it is helpful to get the opinions of members of the public—people who are *not* experts on the subject but who are, or should be, concerned with it. (If a substantial proportion of the public is *not* concerned, that may be a point worth mentioning.)

To get these opinions, be cautious. Many people are unaccustomed to being interviewed. If you pounce on them with direct, thought-provoking questions, they will offer noncommittal answers, or will say they know nothing about the subject.

Indirect methods will give better results. Wherever you meet and talk to people, simply direct the conversation to the subject you are investigating, and notice what people say about it.

For instance, on "Highway Safety," say, "That was a nasty accident out at Fourway Corner last night. Something ought to be done to control these crazy drivers. But what? That's the question."

This will infallibly produce some response.

To find what people think about TV commercials, say something like this: "My brother-in-law just installed one of those switches to cut off the sound during commercials. I wonder how many people use those things."

In this kind of interviewing, you would spoil the effect by whipping out pen and notebook to record the answers you get. But do make your notes as soon as you can. Try to recall the exact words that people use; incorporate them in your notes and, when you make your speech, read a few of the most impressive ones verbatim.

There is no ethical objection to quoting such speakers without their knowledge, since you do not identify them by name. Simply indicate the sex, age and, if relevant, the occupation or social position, of the informant.

"A mother of four children said . . ."

"An unemployed laborer told me . . ."

"A seventeen-year-old girl remarked that . . ."

Use this method freely: it gives immediacy and extra interest to your speeches.

Surveys

Politicians, writers, advertisers and manufacturers often use surveys to find what people think about various subjects. You can conduct surveys to get information for your speeches. Simply draw up a questionnaire, make copies of it, and pass them out to the people whose opinions you want.

Some people will not reply. But from those who do, you may get more accurate answers than you would get by interviewing. The respondent has taken time to think about the subject; to put his thoughts in writing, he has been obliged to clarify and condense them.

If you cannot arrange to collect the completed questionnaires, give each person a stamped, addressed envelope in which to mail his reply to you.

Your surveys, in some respects, can be more helpful than published surveys which cover more people than you could reach.

Your own survey tells you what people in your own neighborhood think about a subject. Moreover, the results of commercial surveys are necessarily days or weeks out of date by the time they are published. Your survey can bring in answers up to a few minutes before you begin to speak.

Library Research

Get acquainted with the resources of your public library. Browse around to see what is available, particularly in your own fields of interest.

Reference books. The encyclopedia is a good place to look first, when you start to investigate a subject. A big library has several different encyclopedias. Consult them all; there may be important differences in the information they offer. Look at old editions of encyclopedias for earlier facts and theories. Consult supplementary yearbooks for recent information.

Atlases, directories, and almanacs are helpful. So are biographical reference books of the *Who's Who* type.

There are specialized annual directories and reference books for most trades, professions, arts and sciences.

Newspaper clipping files. Many libraries have vast collections of newspaper clippings, leaflets and small pamphlets, classified by subjects. These files are a useful second stage of research into a subject. They may contain information more recent than that in the reference books. (But remember that, since newspapers are published in haste, their information is not always reliable.)

Books. Learn to use the book indexes to find books by subject, author or title. Also browse through the shelves; you may occasionally find a book that is not listed in the card index.

Periodical indexes. These are bound volumes that show what magazine articles have been written on any subject. They will lead you to the library's collection of back issues of magazines. Magazine material is generally more reliable than that in newspapers.

Librarians. The main inquiry desk of a large library will direct you to departmental librarians who are specialists in their own subjects. Librarians are eager to give help if you are sensible and tactful in your requests.

Notes. Take notes continuously as you do your library research. It is not enough to write down the facts; you must know where you found them. Note book title, author and page; magazine title, date and page; newspaper title and date.

Personal Reference Library

Several excellent almanacs and annual reference books are published cheaply in paper covers. It is useful to have some of these at home. Keep previous years' issues.

When you read newspapers and magazines, clip and file items you think will be useful. Write on each clipping its source and date of publication.

Collect quotations, anecdotes and striking illustrations for use in your speeches. Buy books on subjects that interest you. Don't overlook the bargains available in second-hand bookstores.

You will not, of course, equal the resources of your public library, but you do not need to cover as much ground. As you do more and more speaking, you probably will find that you specialize on one subject, or a few subjects. On your special subjects you can easily and cheaply accumulate a valuable mass of reference material that, in some ways, is more useful than the library. At the library you often find that someone has borrowed the book you need, and that you must wait a month to get hold of it. Or you may find that an envelope of newspaper clippings has been misfiled so that you cannot read up on the subject you want. Your own material, on the other hand, is instantly available any time you want it.

Building and using your own specialized reference library goes a long way toward making you *an authority* on the subjects of your choice.

Used Speeches

Don't throw away the research notes or the speech notes for speeches you have delivered. File them; they will lighten the labor of preparing the next speech on the same subject, or on a related subject. Or you may have the chance to deliver the same speech, slightly modified, to a new audience.

How Much Research?

Don't be content to gather just enough material to fill out your speech. Get more information than you think you will need.

The possession of abundant information gives you a feeling of confidence that is communicated to your audience, and so helps to make the speech successful. Extra information enables you to answer questions with authority, and also swells your reference files, which will be useful for future speeches.

Summary

Research adds authority to your speeches.
Useful research methods:
    Personal investigation—take notes as you go.
    Formal interview—the opinions of an expert.
    Informal interview—ask the man in the street.
    Surveys—localized, up-to-date results.
    Library research—the world's knowledge.
    Personal reference library—specialized on pet subjects.
    File used research and speech notes.
Ample research builds your self-confidence.
Research is a process of self-education.

Exercise

Take a subject that interests you, but on which you have little information. Research until you can deliver an authoritative speech on it.

Appendix. Ideas for Practical Work

If you are forming a group without a teacher in order to study and practice public speaking, these ideas will help make your meetings enjoyable and profitable. If you are a teacher, conducting classes in public speaking, this appendix can save you time and effort.

The Practice Room

A public speaking class should, if possible, be held in a big room—the bigger the better. The living room of a house is too small. A school classroom is about the smallest that will give good results. An auditorium is better, even if you have only a few participants.

The bigger the room, the sooner the students will learn to speak loudly. A big room also keeps the speaker and his audience well separated. The public speaker must get used to this separation. In a school classroom, the audience should occupy the back rows in order to get them as far as possible from the speaker. In an auditorium the audience at first should be twenty to thirty feet from the speaker; week by week they should move farther away, until they are at the back.

Having the audience well away from the speaker offers another advantage. Some students are disconcerted by the gaze of the audience. This effect is reduced when the audience is farther away, because then the speaker cannot see their eyes so distinctly.

221

A living room is acoustically dead, whereas a big room has some echo. Speakers must get used to the echo. A big room offers space for visitors to augment the audience occasionally when students have progressed far enough to display their skill.

If possible, use a room with a platform; it allows the student to get accustomed to being above his audience.

If possible, have a table or lectern on the platform. The beginner feels horribly exposed at first, and gains in confidence if he can take partial shelter behind a piece of furniture. As self-confidence develops, he can come out from behind the lectern and speak on the open platform.

There should be five chairs on the platform.

The Practice Schedule

Weekly sessions are best, so that students have time to research and plan their speeches.

Sessions should be long enough to give each student at least one three-minute speech. It is better if you can allow ten minutes' speaking time for each student. At first, this should be split into several short speeches; later on, students may use all their time-allowance on one speech.

Practical Work

Formality

Practical work should prepare students to speak confidently and effectively outside the classroom, so the proceedings should be formal, like a public meeting. No matter if students and instructor are on familiar terms outside, they should not be familiar during the sessions.

While practical work is being done, the instructor or one of the students should *act the role* of chairman, and the students should *act the roles* of speakers and spectators at a public meeting.

In other words, practice sessions are *rehearsals* of what students will do when they have to speak in earnest. The more realistic those rehearsals are, the more beneficial they will be.

Nobody benefits if the instructor says, "All right, Jack, I guess you may as well lead off with whatever you've managed to prepare. I know it can't be much, the kind of social life you're leading nowadays."

It is better for the instructor or the student-chairman to say, "Ladies and Gentlemen, the first speaker, for this part of the program, is Mr. Jack Jones. He will speak on the subject of Preserving Our National Parks. Mr. Jack Jones."

Each speaker, when formally announced, should begin with a formal salutation, and generally conduct himself as if he were at a large public meeting. The audience should applaud each speaker when he finishes.

Calling Up Speakers

A useful procedure is to call students to the platform four at a time. Let them sit facing the audience, and call each to speak in turn. This system has four advantages:

1. It gives each student more practice in facing an audience. Although three-quarters of this period is spent listening to other speakers, it still helps to build confidence.

2. It gets students accustomed to the common procedure of having several speakers on the platform.

3. It gives more confidence to the person who is speaking. With four other people near him, he feels less exposed and less nervous than if only he and the chairman were on the platform.

4. It saves time. In a big class, several minutes of each session can be wasted if each student walks to and from the platform alone.

Taking the Chair

As soon as possible, get students to take turns being chairman. The chairman will call on those who are to speak. In a night school class, members may not at first know each other's names; so give the chairman the class register.

Four or five students can take the chair during one session.

With a student in the chair, the instructor is free to sit at the back of the room where he can best judge the practice sessions.

Big Classes

If possible, every student should deliver a prepared speech at every session, but in a big class, where there is not time for everyone to do that, divide the students into several groups. Then a typical session could go like this:

Group A rotate the chairmanship during the session.

Group B give short introductions.

Group C give the main prepared speeches.

Group D ask questions of the speakers.

Group E thank the main speakers.

Frequent Sessions

If sessions are held more often than once a week, students may not be able to prepare a speech every time. Then alternate prepared speeches with various unprepared speaking exercises:

Read a newspaper clipping and comment on it.

Make an impromptu speech on a given subject.

Debate a given subject, with five minutes of preparation.

Have a panel discussion, with five minutes of preparation.

Reading exercises for breath, voice, phrasing and expression.

Time Limits

Speaking to the time limit is important. Insist on this from the first. A kitchen timer is the best way to keep time. The instructor does not have to keep looking at his watch; he can pay full attention to the speaker. Moreover, any annoyance the speaker feels at being cut off by the bell is directed against the timer, not the instructor.

Reading

Usually a few students will try reading or memorizing their speeches with the excuse that they are too nervous to think as they speak. The instructor can tell them that no one is expected to be perfectly fluent at first; that, if they only *pause long enough,* the thoughts will arrange themselves.

Spare Time

If there is time to spare after the individual speeches, it can be filled by a general discussion. The instructor announces a subject, and students speak from the floor. Maintain formality. The chairman indicates who is to speak. Each speaker stands and begins, "Mr. Chairman . . ." and addresses the chair throughout his speech. There should be no backchat among people on the floor.

Criticism of Practical Work

No Instructor

If you have no instructor, here is an easy way to assess one another's early speeches. Allot points on the following scale:

Salutation: measured, impressive.................Maximum 10
Voice: 1. Power—easily fills the room.............Maximum 10
       2. Clarity—every syllable heard............Maximum 10
       3. Pace—unhurried; good pauses...........Maximum 10
Deportment: erect; facing audience squarely........Maximum 10

                    Possible score   50

This scoring system will do for the first few sessions. At this stage the main thing is to establish the habit of speaking loudly, clearly, slowly and confidently. There is no point in criticizing the structure and style of a speech before those matters have been studied.

Later in the course, when you know how to construct a speech properly, you can use this scoring system:

Voice: clear, varied and pleasing..................Maximum 10
Deportment: posture, gesture, facial expression....Maximum 10
Planning: good selection and arrangement of mate-
   rial ....Maximum 10
Interest: material made relevant to audience........Maximum 10
Persuasiveness: make audience believe, feel, act....Maximum 10

                    Possible score   50

With Instructor

Instructing a class, you can still use the scales given above. Explain the scoring system, and let each student mark every other student's practical work. The idea is not to have the marks read out, or otherwise communicated, but to sharpen the students' awareness of what makes an effective speaker and an effective speech. You can also use these scales as the basis for your spoken comments on speeches.

It is a good idea to let each speaker finish—no matter what faults he is committing—before offering criticism. There are two exceptions to that rule:

1. If he is inaudible, tell him at once to speak up.
2. If he speaks too long, the timer will interrupt him.

If each student can have two practice speeches per session he will learn faster. He can apply in the second speech the suggestions you made to him after the first.

Exercises

Here are some additional exercises that can be done profitably during class sessions.

Relaxation

In early sessions, students may be fearful and tense. The relaxation exercises in Chapter 10 can be done before beginning practical work.

Speech Planning

Toward the end of the course, when students can confidently deliver a planned speech, let them practice modifying the plan. Make them lengthen, shorten or otherwise adapt their speeches at a few minutes' notice.

Audience Analysis

To emphasize the need for suiting the speech to the audience, try planning speeches for different audiences. For example, say,

"Next week we'll imagine you are going to speak to such-and-such an audience. Plan your speech, and deliver it, to appeal to that kind of audience."

Self-Confidence

There may be a student who is so nervous that he simply can't say a word when he faces the audience. Don't let him get down without speaking. Make him begin with his back to the audience. After delivering a few speeches in that position, he can stand sideways to the audience for a while. Next, let him stand at a 45-degree angle, away from the audience. Finally he will be able to speak facing the audience squarely.

Breathing

One or more breathing exercises from Chapter 9 can be done in class sessions. They are recommended because:

1. They increase students' lung capacity.

2. They tend to keep students more alert. Particularly in evening classes when members may be tired, deep breathing refreshes them.

3. It is good to form the habit of doing a breathing exercise before speaking.

Articulation

Here are some more articulation exercises. An interesting way to use them is to give each student a piece of paper with three of the sentences typed on it. Let each in turn stand with his back to the audience (that makes the exercise harder) and read one sentence. Ask another student to repeat what he has said. (This tests A's articulation, and gives B some practice in articulation, too.) Do the same with the second and third sentences, then give another student a turn.

Cat-like acrobat snaps neck in eighty-foot drop.

"Don't rock boat" begs desperate Deputy Prime Minister.

Coats, hats and bags lost in checkroom collapse.

Sink and drainboard demolished as kids dynamite cupboard.

Sadist killed dogs and cats: "Loved sight of red blood."

Battered trunk held secret stock of ten-cent stamps.
Abandoned campsite contained corpses of eight scouts.
Great orator's last words: "I can't articulate."
Bullet-riddled diamond magnate discovered in blood-stained bed.
Heartsick parent punished for neglect of eight tots.
Two-hundred-pound brute beat up mate in late-night street fight.
Unnoticed rust spot stopped clock striking midnight.
Rotted stumps make teeth ache, says eminent Greek dentist.
"She trumped my ace" pleads bridge champ on assault rap.
Redhead demonstrated twist in court: condemned as indecent.
Parents protest hot rod craze: kids won't stop it.
Wife's kiss rouses concussion patient from six-week trance.
Weaver makes translucent glass cloth twice as soft as silk.
Twenty vandals vent their spite on cast-iron cemetery
monuments.
Former singer succumbs silently to deep-seated abdominal
tumor.
Black-clad mourners sob as choir intones sad funeral hymn.
Sick detective leaps from bed to nab much-wanted con man.
Woodshed discipline needed today, says centenarian granddad.
Stolen gem found in sealed two-pound can of damson jam.
Stickup artist, chased by victim, fell down deep sewer manhole.
Mystery man remains ten hours alone in dimly-lit living room.
Strychnine kills champion Dalmatian in double-locked kennel.
Black-masked gunman wounds nine, then evades hot police
pursuit.

Introducing a Speaker

1. Pair the students off. One week A introduces B, who makes
a prepared speech. Next week, vice versa.

2. Get a visitor in, and let the class interview him to prepare
introductions for an imaginary speech by him.

3. Let class interview the instructor, to prepare introductions
for a speech by him.

Impromptu Speaking

1. Give each speaker a short newspaper clipping. Let him read
it and then speak on it for two or three minutes.

2. Let each student write on a piece of paper a subject for an impromptu speech. Put the papers in a hat. Let each in turn draw a subject and speak on it for two or three minutes.

A useful routine for these exercises:

1. Student A receives his subject and is given two minutes to think about it.

2. Just before A begins to speak, student B receives his subject. While A is speaking, B plans what he will say.

3. Just before B begins to speak, C receives his subject, and so on.

This gives a fair imitation of actual impromptu speaking conditions—preparing the speech while the previous speaker is on his feet.

(A good follow-up exercise is to have each student take this week's impromptu subject and prepare a speech on it for next week.)

Speech Subjects

There is a list of speech subjects at the end of Chapter 3. Each of them is broad enough to provide themes for half a dozen speeches. Here are some more subjects:

The garbage problem.

Juvenile delinquency.

Noise—its dangers and means of control.

Safety measures for swimmers. (A persuasive speech)

Emotional immaturity and dangerous driving.

The telephone—servant or tyrant?

Police power and personal freedom.

Incurable disease: the doctor's responsibility.

What is a friend?

The dog—man's best friend or worst pest?

The pleasures of reading.

Self-inflicted diseases.

Flying saucers: fact or fiction?

My most frightening experience.

If I were dictator for a day.

My ideal vacation.

TV and human happiness.

What I would do with a million dollars.

Speaking the truth.

Alcoholism.
Life in the year 2000.
Easy credit: blessing or menace?
The rights of animals.
Arbitration of industrial disputes.
Public regulation of radio & TV broadcasting.
Religion and politics.
Compulsory voting in public elections.
Corporal punishment for violent crime.
The jury system.
Public lotteries.
Professional sports.
War crimes and criminals.
Reform of the universities.
My favorite fictional character.
My hometown.
If I had three wishes.
My favorite historical character.
(Note that the "lonely-hearts" columns in the daily newspapers provide an inexhaustible mine of up-to-date, controversial subjects.)

Subjects for Debate

Government should prohibit the marriage of people with hereditary diseases.

Teaching of foreign languages should be compulsory in high schools.

We are wiser and happier than our parents were at our age.

Church property and income should be taxed.

We have no right to civilize so-called undeveloped peoples.

All forms of gambling should be legalized.

School holidays are too long.

All censorship laws should be repealed.

Honesty is the best policy.

Woman's place is in the home.

The police need more power to fight crime.

Big cities have too much political power.

The calendar should be reformed.

The closed shop should be prohibited.

Modern civilization is degenerating.
Euthanasia should be available to all who want it.
Every war should be fought as a total war.

Subjects for Panel Discussion

Is life worth living?
What do we require in order to be happy?
Sex discrimination in employment and politics.
How much welfare can the country afford?
What do we expect from education?
Health—a personal or a public responsibility?
Have governments got too much power?
Inter-racial friction—is there a cure?
Wilderness parks—how should they be regulated?
Hunting—sport or sadism?
What causes crime?
Marijuana and L.S.D.—should their use be banned?
Should Sunday be a day of rest and worship?
Government subsidy of the arts.
What future for religion in a secular society?
The changing parent-child relationship.
Does mass advertising benefit or harm the public?
Should we always obey the law?
Is coeducation a good thing?

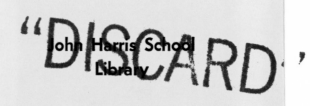